Young Heroes

A Learner's Guide to End Human Trafficking

The Reader!

Copyright © 2014, 2012 Kurt Hoffman. All rights reserved.

Young Heroes: A Learner's Guide to End Human Trafficking – The Reader! published in the United States by Drummer Boy Books and Media, LLC: October, 2014. No part of this publication may be reproduced or transmitted in any form or by any means, electronic or mechanical, including photocopy, recording or by any information storage and retrieval system now known or to be invented, without permission in writing from the publisher.

Young Heroes Books, an Imprint of Drummer Boy Books and Media, LLC

Hoffman, Kurt, 1979-
Young Heroes: A Learner's Guide to End Human Trafficking / written by Kurt Hoffman;
edited by Angela Jurgensen, Kelly Berthelot.

Includes bibliographical references and index.
Also available in electronic format.
ISBN 978-0-9907076-0-8 (bound)
ISBN 978-0-9907076-1-5 (paperback)

United States Library of Congress Control Number: 2014916977

1. Slavery--Juvenile literature. 2. Human trafficking--Juvenile literature. 3. Anti-slavery movements--Citizen participation--Juvenile literature. 4. Human trafficking--Prevention--Citizen participation--Juvenile literature. 5. Philosophy--Juvenile literature.
6. Social issues--Self-Esteem & Self-Reliance--Juvenile literature.
7. Social issues--delinquency prevention--Juvenile literature. I. Title.

Thank you to Becky Ankeny for your amazing design work and selflessness. Thank you to Jonas and Treat Photography for letting us use their beautiful photos. Thank you to all the photographers who contribute to Morguefile.com, from where we sourced many of our pictures. Thank you to Kevin Bales and Anti-Slavery International for letting us use some of their touching images. Thank you to the Arizona League to End Regional Trafficking for the photo donations. Thank you Angela and Dean for giving your lives to something bigger than yourselves.

Foreword by Dr. Kevin Bales.

Our editing team dedicates this book to the memory of the talented, funny and kind young editor, Kelly Berthelot, whose journey on this Earth ended far too soon. This is the last book project Kelly completed; she poured her soul into it, as with everything she touched. We hope this book helps many people, and that it becomes a changing force, as she believed it could be.
We miss you, Kelly

Printed and bound in the USA on acid-free paper that contains
no material from old-growth forests, using ink that is safe for children.

Young Heroes

A Learner's Guide to End Human Trafficking

The Reader!

Kurt Hoffman

Young Heroes Books
An Imprint of Drummer Boy Books and Media

For Korah. You are the strongest, most selfless person I know, and you make life so awesome it is ridiculous.

In memory of Chris. Your life changed mine.

Young Heroes Manifesto

1. **We live the examined life** - by testing our assumptions, beliefs, and values we ensure they are objectively good for us as dignified human persons.

2. **We are teachable** and humbly seek truth above all else.

3. **We work diligently to have integrity** in and between our thoughts, desires, words, and actions.

4. **We cultivate our unique talents** and joyfully serve others with them.

5. **We live simply, steward the earth, and consume thoughtfully.**

6. **We are justice-seekers** who stand for the truth that all humans have equal value, dignity, rights, and responsibilities regardless of gender, race, ethnicity, or any other natural diversity that make us beautifully awesome.

7. **We are mercy givers** who recognize ourselves as works in progress needing patience, forgiveness, and room to mature into the thoughtful creators of culture we are becoming.

TABLE OF CONTENTS

i.	Introducing the Young Heroes!	2
ii.	The Attitude of a Young Hero	3
iii.	Goals for Young Heroes	3
iv.	Values for Young Heroes	4
v.	Directions for Young Heroes	6
V.	Tips for Facilitators	7
vi.	Knowledge	8
1.	Splitting Hairs : Defining Slavery	9
2.	Through the Trees : A Look at the History of Slavery	23
3.	It's Not You, It's Me : A New Kind of Slavery	36
4.	Devil's in the Details : How Trafficking Works	47
5.	Life in Funhouse Mirrors : How Modern-day Slaves are Used	59
6.	Numbers are Like Bears : Statistics on Human Trafficking	70
7.	Because the TV Said So, Dang! : A Look Into Supply and Demand	84
8.	More Moves Than a B-Boy : The Birthing of a Global Abolitionist's Movement	96
Appendix I	- 20 Forms of Action	108
Appendix II	- Reason : A Comprehensive Definition	110
References		112
Shout-Outs!		116
About the Author		117

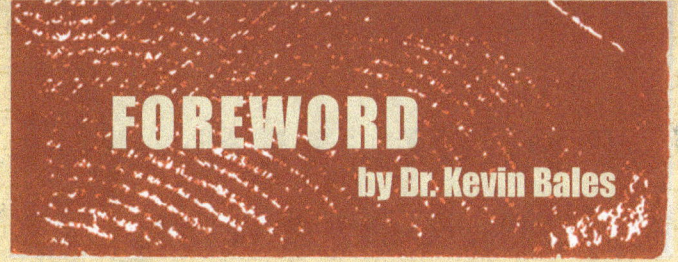

FOREWORD
by Dr. Kevin Bales

Too many people talk down to youth. I knew this when I was a teenager; I know this now from my sixteen-year-old son. There's a crazy idea out there that somehow the internet has made young people lazy and dumb, but it's not true. The internet is like having the biggest library and archive and museum at your fingertips anytime you want it. It means that young people, who take time to look, now know more that previous generations could ever have known.

One of the things young people today know is not new; they just understand it better than any previous generation. *They know that the generations that went before them have left them a world that is a mess.* I knew this when I was sixteen, but without the world's knowledge at my fingertips on the web, I never knew just how big the problem was. Today young people get to know everything in detail, and they have to deal with new kinds of issues. One issue that this generation understands better than their parents and grandparents is slavery.

How do you deal with an Earth that is such a mess? What are you supposed to do with the knowledge that slavery exists in our world in spite of the fact that it is illegal everywhere and universally seen as morally repugnant? And then how do you fit slavery together with other challenges – global warming, species loss, ethnic and religious conflicts, and HIV-AIDS to name just a few? Some people, young and old, will deal with all this by giving up, getting distracted, getting wasted. Others will want to act. They will want to do something because they do not want to live in a world with slavery and global warming and don't see why they should. But what action should they take?

It may sound odd, but the most important action to fix this mess is to stop and think. So many of the problems we're all facing exist because people didn't think. Blinded by greed or ideology or ego, people just pushed ahead and didn't think through the consequences or their actions. All of us who are alive today, and especially young people, just have to be smarter than that. We have to know how to think; we have to build a toolbox in our heads full of very sharp ideas. We have to learn how to debunk the nonsense advertisers and politicians want to feed us, to keep us from thinking clearly. We have to take the whole world into our minds and then imagine it better.

That's where this book comes in. Kurt Hoffman and team have written a user's manual for the toolbox in your brain. Your brain may ache a little as you use this book, but that's good: like a muscle, it is getting stronger. Things that were confusing or complex or daunting will become clear. Ideas that used to wriggle around in your head like eels will become balls that your mind can juggle. No one can ever take this toolbox away from you – and that's power. Think of Gandhi -- he was stripped of everything, suppressed and locked in a jail, but he had his toolbox. His mind sent out ideas that rolled over his country and the world like a tsunami, changing lives. You can, too.

- Dr. Kevin Bales, Author of Disposable People, Co-founder of Free the Slaves

As an author, a professor of sociology, and consultant to the United Nations Global Program on Human Trafficking, Kevin Bales is one of the world's foremost experts on modern slavery. He is the co-founder of Free the Slaves, a nonprofit whose brilliant website is packed with facts and inspirations to action.

If you like this reader, you will love the full-length version. It has:

- Three times as many pages
- Twice as many chapters
- 16 Step-by-step Action Tanks that empower readers to develop their own forms of action
- Five whole chapters on becoming abolitionists
- And much (much!) more

Get your copy at: drummerboybooksandmedia.com

For a limited time use promo code, "Big Deal" to secure a 15% discount!!

INTRODUCING
The Young Heroes!
Drum roll please ...

Who: Human beings

Age: 13 - 100 (Seriously, adults should read this too)

Where: High, Home, and Charter schools, organizations, group homes, churches, living rooms, libraries, detention centers, coffee shops, on trains, street corners, or while sitting under trees.

Background: All

The focus of this *Reader!* version of *Young Heroes: A Learner's Guide to End Human Trafficking* is to educate, empower, and **inspire** young people to abolish modern-day slavery. Though we hope readers of all ages will benefit from this book, it has been specifically developed for readers between the ages of 13 and 18, an ideal age for gaining awareness of social issues. We want to build a foundation that will help eradicate injustices in the world while challenging readers to examine their deepest selves. This is not a book designed to tell readers how and what to think, but instead one that presents an array of ideas and invitations for readers to think critically and live life to its fullest.

Young people in developed countries have some amazing and historically unique gifts. Today, they are more mobile and independent than any other generation, having been globally connected from a young age through technologies such as the Internet, cell phones, and airplanes. They possess the unique potential to celebrate diversity, having grown up in classrooms mixed by gender, ethnicity, and culture. Topping that, today's youth are also said to be uniquely self-motivated, willing to break molds, take roads less traveled, and fight for noble causes.

Human trafficking, on the other hand, is a complex global problem, and violates every bit of human rights. To overcome such evil, we need people who are innovative, appreciate human diversity, and are in tune with the world's newest technologies; it is clear, when considering the strengths of our youth, that with the right guidance they are best equipped to eventually abolish slavery and human trafficking.

While some young people might say they are confused, and others are finding their way, all are full of awesome potential. By combining education, self-awareness, and empowerment, this curriculum is designed to reach youth where they are, while also calling them to something higher. It is our goal to counteract pop culture's misdirection and youth's confusion by harnessing their strengths. By focusing on a common goal we can promote unity.

Abolishing slavery is a tough job, but someone has to do it. Whether you are a parent, teacher, or a young person reading this, please know today's youth are unique, powerful, and have what it takes. To all: listen, learn, and question everything—not just because you want to raise contradiction, but for the sake of finding the right answers. Let's work together and go big. Let's help our children reach their potential as people, and bring to life our hope to abolish slavery once and for all. Let's prepare for the future and prepare our *Young Heroes*.

The Attitude of a Young Hero

Young Heroes Books' works from a unique perspective. A young hero does not come from the political left or right; a young hero has no hidden agendas. Rather, a young heroes aim must be to bring forth nothing more or less than the truth in every area of life—to know how things really are, not just how we want them to be or how we assume them to be. Further, young heroes must seek to be fully alive, active, and always cultivating the good and trumping the evil in the world and even within our very selves.

Life is a journey, and we are all pilgrims. While you know some things, you do not know all things; you must always be teachable. As learners in this process known as the human experience, we must believe life's complexities can be sorted out. We must know that life's most important things can be sought, obtained, cultivated, and shared. Further, we must also trust all humans have a common ground and that unity is an achievable goal. Our lives and our world are destined to get better and better, not worse and worse, or to remain stagnant. This should be our attitude, and how you choose to carry yourself. Never settle for less.

As humans, we are not perfect, but we should not use this as an excuse to slack off or ignore the suffering in our world. Rather, despite our imperfections, we should be able to acknowledge the needs of others as well as our need for others. In our interconnected world, we all need each other—not only those alive today, but also those in the generations to come, as well as the ones before us, who we can learn so much from. Summed up, changing the world begins with changing yourself.

Goals For Young Heroes

The goal of this book can be summed up in two words: Abolish slavery. But this is no simple task and will not be possible without a solid alternative in its place. In our case, human flourishing is that alternative. For these reasons, the goals for our readers also include vibrantly living the examined life, exponentially increasing self-awareness, and cultivating understanding of the most basic elements of the human experience and human nature. The specific elements, for example, that identify all human persons as equal, and thus, when highlighted, prove slavery is universally wrong. Systematically building on that, we hope for millions of young people to cultivate their human potential, develop their unique talents, and join together in the common pursuit of truth, justice, human dignity, and freedom for every single slave worldwide.

Values For Young Heroes

Thoughtfulness is critical if you are to leave a positive legacy in this world. Be willing to self-examine, turn from bad ideas, and think critically about social norms—you must promote questions, not run from them.

Integrity means consistency between what you say and do. If you begin by searching for consistency, you can then thoughtfully gain integrity. A lack of integrity is one of the reasons why slavery exists, so it is no small thing. While it is hard to be consistent, if you make it a habit you will grow more and more into a person of integrity.

Humility means you can see where you stop and the world begins. Each of us knows some things, but no human knows all things; remember to listen. You are to be humble, realize how little you know, and live aware of how much you depend on others.

Knowledge is the key to a meaningful life. The better you understand the world you live in and how you fit into it, the better your life will be. By the same token, the better you understand human nature and the human condition, the better you will know and advocate for truth over falsehood. So you must always be ready to learn, and be willing to self-examine. This means you must also be willing to admit what you don't know or understand, and always ask lots of questions.

Discernment is a virtue often lost. You must value this because it is a vital skill, as it allows you to see the difference between what's meaningful and meaningless, true and false, good and evil, as well as right and wrong.

Community is the sense you have of belonging to a place based on its ideas, location, and the people around you. No person is an island; your community provides a safe place for you to have a voice, participate in decisions, contribute, and experience heartfelt connections with others. Being a part of your community means that you can share your ideas and educate people about social issues. In a community, the voice of one can quickly become the voice of many.

Empowerment gives your voice strength to speak out against injustices and the evil you see in the world. We all need strength, awareness, and confidence to reach our potential and to achieve our goals. Becoming empowered usually happens with the help of others, through encouragement and consistency. True empowerment must be both personal and community-wide; there is much more power in numbers.

Support is foundational to any person trying to change the status quo, or trying to right a wrong. Giving and receiving support is essential to any community. It is necessary if you are to grow and endure hardships, and it also helps you see life from diverse angles. Life cannot be lived alone; we need one another. Through support, your talents and strengths are shared, and you can accomplish much more than you could ever do alone.

Responsibility acknowledges that at the end of every day you are accountable for your beliefs, values, choices, feelings, and actions. Mistakes that you make must be accounted for, and corrected; by the same token, your good deeds are also your responsibility. As a human being you have rights that others should respect, and you must acknowledge your responsibility to treat others the same way.

Innovation allows for new ideas, individual creativity, and imagination to flourish. Being innovative, seizing opportunities, and thinking big is critical for you to reach your goals. By recognizing that many of your fellow humans lack opportunities to be innovative and improve things, you begin to value the opportunities that you are given, and can commit to being good stewards of these opportunities.

Equality is a very important reality for you to uphold. Equality should be honored while diversity is celebrated. Each of our journeys tells a story, and therefore has value. Affirming human equality invites each member to contribute, which invariably brings unity.

Trust is built through the group's openness and by living with integrity. It involves having faith in one another, and in your ability to fulfill your potential. Trust rejects indifference while promoting confidentiality and privacy. Focus on being honest in words and actions, because this is necessary for dialogue and building lasting relationships. It reflects respect for yourself and others.

Self-Awareness is critical. To say you are aware of the world when you are not yet aware of yourself leads to a dangerous path; lack of self-awareness causes one to only follow others' thoughts, or react to others' actions. By cultivating self-awareness, you can choose the thoughts you have, and ensure that they are consistent with the things you say and the actions you take.

Self-examination and a young hero go together like peanut butter and jelly. By becoming aware of your strengths and weaknesses, you may find things about yourself that need to be developed, strengthened, and even changed. Be it ideas, beliefs, desires, behaviors, habits, lifestyle, culture, feelings, friends, or anything else inside you, self-examination will help you figure out where your strengths lie, and how to use these strengths to become the change you want to see in the world.

Serving others is not only a choice you make, but it is also a way of life. Whether directly or indirectly, you must seek to ease your fellow person's burden. It is your responsibility to serve others with your talents, and it should also be your joy.

Being Accountable is something many people seek to avoid. You, however, must recognize how quickly you can change, which is why you should find people who can hold you to your word and not let you fall short of your potential. Respect the opinion of your parents or guardians, and always try to follow the correct path towards the truly good life.

Flexibility is a value because everyone's situation and circumstances differ. We must each be flexible with ourselves and with each other, as some will catch on quicker than others within any given part of this book. Be ready to adapt and change things along the way, keeping in mind learning and growing are always the main goals.

Human Dignity must be upheld. At the most basic level, you should value all people because all deserve the same love and respect. Regardless of any differences they may present from your culture, sex, skin color, country of birth, or even preferences, all humans deserve dignity. Remember to respect yourself and your body through the choices you make; you must uphold the human dignity of everyone around you, starting with yourself.

Gratitude is a positive attitude all of us must seek to have. While people remain imperfect and the world suffers injustice, you must still remain positive and grateful for all that is good, true, and beautiful in your life, in others, and in your world. Evil exists, but so does good, and for that you should be thoroughly grateful.

Directions for Young Heroes

This *Reader!* version of *Young Heroes: A Learner's Guide to End Human Trafficking* is a creative and interactive resources attempting to reach across cultures and school popularity lines to tap into your strengths and talents. You will find throughout each chapter written portions geared to inform and challenge your intellect in different ways. You will become familiar with the many types of learning, and this will give you a chance to discover your natural learning style and harness your individual strengths.

This *Reader!* version of *Young Heroes: A Learner's Guide to End Human Trafficking* is designed to be a flexible resource for young people but is also very accessible to older audiences. Within each of the eight chapters you will find different learning features aimed to increase your understanding of human trafficking, of yourself, and of the world at large. The more seriously you take these academic features, the more you will benefit from this book and the better you can help make the world a better place. **If you want something even meatier get the full-version.** *Young Heroes: A Learner's Guide to End Human Trafficking* **has eight more chapters, Action Tanks, hundreds more resource, and nearly three times as many pages!**

Themes are different for each chapter. Look out for unique quotations, images, pictures of abolitionists, and art styles to bring the message home. If you are a visual learner, use the graphics as discussion topics or to journal about.

Questions are asked to get you to think about each topic. In each chapter you will find five multiple-choice, true/false, or essay questions. Be sure to answer them. Some will be related to what you have just learned, while others are more personal and opinion based. In both cases, shoot for the most honest answer.

Key Words will be in **bold** throughout each chapter. You will have to define these words using a dictionary, or the Internet. Be sure to write down the definitions on the journal pages at the end of each chapter. This will help you become more used to seeking for the meaning of things. Do this also with any other words you come across and don't understand.

Creation Tanks are designed to engage your creative side, benefit from web-based resources, and encourage the examination of pop-culture. Ranging from listening to music and speeches, to watching videos and movies, specific directions will be offered in each chapter.

Think Tanks challenge you by offering deeper ideas, promoting critical thinking on each chapter. For homework, each Think Tank assigns you a task that will be a lot of fun: you must hunt down and locate at least one new resource that discusses the topic given. It can be a book, something from the Internet, or a person you talk to, but you should write down what it is and where you found it. Reflecting on the topic, finish by writing your thoughts about the given subject. Your reflection should be at least five sentences in length and have at least one reference to the resource you found.

Field Journaling will help you develop your skills in reflection and grow in knowledge. Using the journal pages provided in the end of each chapter, write down thoughts and feelings that come up as you go. Feel comfortable to agree or disagree with what you read, take notes on what you don't understand, or make additional observations. Your thoughts matter, so pour your heart out; express yourself through writing, poetry or drawings. This section is like two for the price of one: it will also help you get comfy with living a young hero's life, so be sure to take note of convictions or beliefs you hold as well.

The Memoirs of a Young Hero section creates room for self-exploration and self-examination. You can respond to the questions in a journal-type format. Also, there is a 1–10 scale for you to rate yourself on how well you support or live out the concepts discussed within the chapters. At the end of the book, reread all of your Memoir entries, along with the rest of your journal. Rewriting this as a self-narrative will make it easier to know yourself better, including your talents and how to serve others with them.

Abolitionists Research: A name and picture of a notable abolitionist are given at the beginning of each chapter. While the details of these people could have been provided too, it is more beneficial for you to research them and jot down some facts about each one. Let it be a meaningful journey into the lives of another, and practice putting yourself into their shoes. Journal about what it would have been like to live their lives.

Tips for Facilitators

Some intentional benefits of this book are that it is portable, adaptable, and flexible. While we offer a variety of ideas and options for both individual and group work, please feel free to be creative. You know your specific audience better than we do, so come up with your own exercises and feel free to have students create assignments or complete only some – it's your call. The most important thing is that your students gain two primary cornerstones: a greater knowledge about slavery and human trafficking, and learn to be challenged intellectually about their potential greatness, personal values and goals in life. Yes, these are big and even touchy topics but also critical for young minds. The choices all of us adults made as young people affect us today, for better or worse; the same is true for today's young people. This is why the more they get to know what they are as a group, who they are as individuals, and what they are capable of as a generation, the better off our whole world will be.

Much of the information in this book and the academic angles it works from may be foreign to you as well. If not, great; but if so, don't sweat it. Consider working through it yourself before the students do, take advantage of all related resources, and then just do the best you can – which, for sure, will be pretty amazing! Lastly and most importantly, a deep heartfelt thanks for using this curriculum!

A facilitator's guide is available for download at drummerboybooksandmedia.com.

KNOWLEDGE

Knowledge is our goal.

The definition of knowledge is *that which is believed, true, and justifiable.* Having opinions, beliefs, or unexamined ideas alone, therefore, are not necessarily knowledge. Your ability to discern and grow in knowledge of the world around you—your family, your community, your country— is how you, as a single person, connect to the universe and all the creatures in it.

This is why to do anything well, whether it be music, art, science, or family, we must have *knowledge* of it first. Some might even say that to know and to be known is our deepest longing as humans. In light of our nature, this makes sense. But have you ever wondered how you know anything? And how do you know that you *know*?

Once, people claimed to *know* that the world was flat, when in reality it was not true; they only *believed* it. Even though they sought to justify their beliefs via **common sense logic**, this belief was eventually proven false. As we now know, the world is not flat, but round! In this example, you can see how the quickest way to limit human potential is to think that you have true knowledge of something when in fact you do not. The same is true for every one of us; this is the reason why you should seek real knowledge about the world, about human nature, and about yourself. You must search for **truth,** not mere opinions or theories. So saddle up and get ready!

SPLITTING HAIRS
(DEFINING SLAVERY)

CHAPTER 1

Booker T. Washington

The question "what is man?" is one of the most important questions confronting any generation.
— MLK, The Measure of a Man

Slavery has existed throughout all of human history. Virtually every known ethnic group has both been slaves and enslaved others at some point in time. Now begins your exploration of slavery in order to understand it and to determine once and for all if it is actually wrong or not, and why. To do so, let's start by defining some important terms; the definition of slavery and its core ideas must be grasped, as simply claiming it is wrong without foundation only weakens our final goals. This is where you are encouraged to start thinking critically! Before you start, go to your journal and jot down how you currently define slavery.
Do you think **slavery** is wrong? Why?

Here is how the Merriam-Webster dictionary defines a slave: A person held in servitude as the chattel of another.

Historian and author Milton Meltzer elaborates on this concept: A slave is a man or woman who is property of another and therefore under their authority and power. To have a slave is, "To possess someone, to hold property, which means to have unlimited power over it. The slave is subjected to his master, not just to his authority but also to the full exercise of his master's power. That power has always been used to compel the slave to work. A free laborer can stop working whenever he likes. It may sometime be at the risk of starving, but he can quit. The slave cannot."

Question #1

Circle the answer you think is most true:

A) Slavery is wrong only when the person does not deserve it

B) Slavery is never wrong

C) Slavery is wrong only if the country you live in says it is

D) Slavery is always wrong

E) It totally depends on the situation

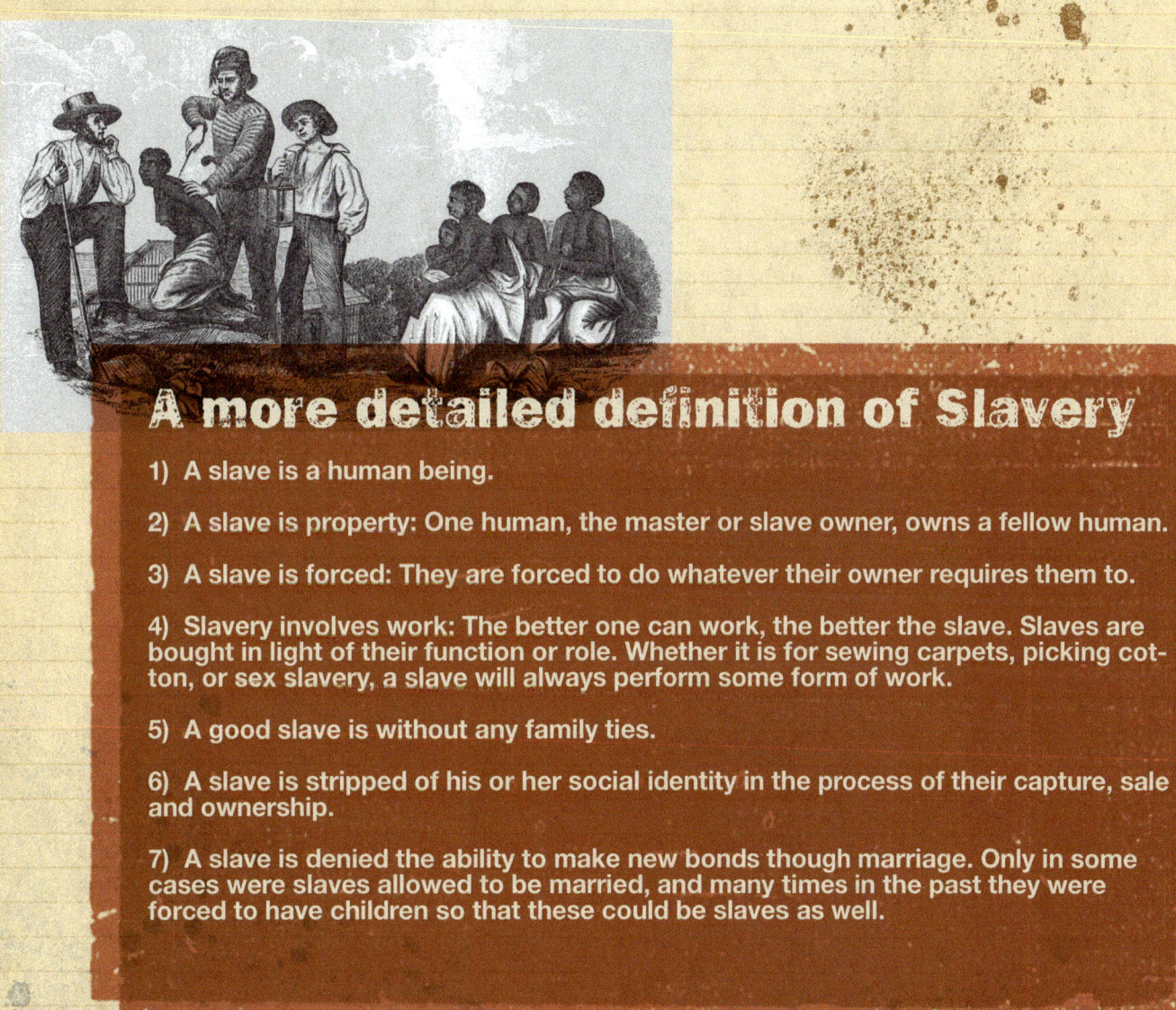

A more detailed definition of Slavery

1) A slave is a human being.

2) A slave is property: One human, the master or slave owner, owns a fellow human.

3) A slave is forced: They are forced to do whatever their owner requires them to.

4) Slavery involves work: The better one can work, the better the slave. Slaves are bought in light of their function or role. Whether it is for sewing carpets, picking cotton, or sex slavery, a slave will always perform some form of work.

5) A good slave is without any family ties.

6) A slave is stripped of his or her social identity in the process of their capture, sale and ownership.

7) A slave is denied the ability to make new bonds though marriage. Only in some cases were slaves allowed to be married, and many times in the past they were forced to have children so that these could be slaves as well.

Two types of slavery

Physical Slavery

The most obvious form of slavery is physical. This means the slaves are physically held against their will, threatened or abused, and forced to work, often enduring gross treatment including being chained or caged, beaten, raped, ridiculed, and forced to go days without food or water. Physical slavery can also include being forced to work in very dangerous situations, such as under water, in mines, or in extreme temperatures. For the slave owners, their goal is to make their slaves as productive as possible, paying little attention to their wellbeing.

Mental Slavery

Mental slavery happens to the human mind. It is possible to be mentally enslaved but not physically enslaved. It is also possible for one to be physically enslaved but not mentally enslaved, however difficult it may seem. It also is possible to be mentally enslaved but not physically enslaved. This is because, in some cases, those enslaved physically can still have the option to be free in their minds. This freedom allows them to dream of better things, design plans for escape, make music, be hopeful, and maintain some degree of self-dignity. In other words, no one can *force* specific thoughts or beliefs onto anyone, but we all choose to accept the beliefs we hold. A slave might say, "You can break my body but you cannot break my spirit."

Former slave Frederick Douglass notices this truth as well when he says in his book, *Narrative of the Life of Frederick Douglass, an American Slave* in 1845:

"I have found that to make a contented slave, it is necessary to make a thoughtless one. It is necessary to darken his moral and mental vision, and, as far as possible, to *annihilate the power of reason*. He must be able to detect no inconsistencies in slavery; he must be made to feel slavery is right; and he can be brought to that only when he ceases to be a man."

In the same way, you can become enslaved mentally by believing falsehoods, which happens by thoughtlessly "going with the flow." So, examining your beliefs and what you hold to be true should be done most critically. For example, "popularity is important," or "I need to have sex to be loved," are commonly held false beliefs among today's young people, which are only exacerbated by the media's influence and reach. These things are not true in reality, even though in your mind they may be held as true. The scariest thing, then, is that a person can actually believe something that is totally false, and yet live as if it's true. Slavery has gone on for this long in great part because masses of people have not examined their beliefs and in turn believed false things.

This is also why the deepest degree of slavery is when one actually believes they deserve it. For example, a slave might be treated like an animal and soon enough believe that he or she is an animal, and therefore deserves to be treated like one. In doing this, slaves stop questioning their purpose in the world, and eventually lose self-dignity and hope.

Question #2

It is possible for a person to be mentally enslaved and not know it.

True   False

Why?

Mental slavery is often self-inflicted, and the root causes are lies. One can become a mental slave to another by believing their lies and manipulation, but this type of slavery can also start on one's own mind. For instance—have you ever told a lie, and then needed to tell another lie to cover up the first one? Sometimes the lying goes on for so long that you can end up becoming a slave to those lies. If you tell different stories to different people, you can get really confused by forgetting who you told the truth to and who you lied to. Make the tough choice of following a path of truth: this is the attitude of one who seeks to be mentally free of slavery.

"I prefer to be true to myself, even at the hazard of incurring the ridicule of others, rather than to be false, and incur my own abhorrence."
—Frederick Douglass, former slave.

Philosophical Questions about Slavery

So far you have read about what slavery *is*. But this is only the first step, as it does not prove it to be right or wrong. This particular discussion has throughout history troubled many people, while others have never seemed to question it. Some of those who have not questioned it—you may be surprised to find out—have gone so far as to provide "proofs" that slavery was good, lawful, and just. Before dwelling further into this book, it is your turn to tell us what you think from the get-go. Is slavery right or wrong? Moral, immoral, or neither? And why do you think that? Write a couple of paragraphs in the journal pages at the back of this chapter.

To answer this question in an informed and philosophical manner, we must dig further into the defining terms. At the end of the day, both the slave and the slave owners are *humans*. This raises a question: what gives one human the right to own a fellow human? Throughout history and to this day, slave owners have used race, gender, age, nationality, wealth, and/or power as a reason for owning slaves. At the furthest degree, some have simply denied these people were, in fact, fully human. They would say the slaves are less evolved, have a different nature, are ungodly, stupid, beastly, and/or mere animals.

What we are faced with, therefore, is a demand to define what a human is before we can show why slavery is wrong. Furthermore, we are also pressed to define the roots of slavery. These, as previously stated, will be found within your conceptions about the reality of the world, ideas about good and evil, and beliefs about human nature. The reason why is this: Our actions reveal what is within us. That is, our beliefs, values, and what we want out of life are revealed by our choices, behaviors, words, and deeds. Exercising slavery is no different; within each person guilty of slavery, three core roots are almost invariably found. The funny thing is, these rotten roots are deformations of human rights and of things everyone searches for in life. These are the desire to have personal pleasure above all else, the desire for praise and validation, and the desire to have power and control over others.

Question #3
To the best of your ability, define the term "human." Ask yourself, what is the main difference between human beings and animals?

Write the answer below.

But don't I have the right to pursue happiness?

First, the corruption of the search for happiness brings *the belief that maximum pleasure, and minimal pain, is the highest good for oneself.* This is the first root of slavery. Pleasure, or happiness, in and of itself is, of course, not an evil; it is a great thing, something we are wired for as humans. Nevertheless, the search of maximum pleasure while suffering a minimum amount of pain in life leads us to see others as tools to be used towards achieving one's self-centered desires at any cost. There are countless examples of this to be found in all cultures; if you feel like it, here is an opportunity to start doing some field research in your own culture! More on this in the Case Study on the next page and Think Tank on page 30.

But isn't it okay I desire to be loved?

Like happiness, there is of course nothing wrong with desiring to be loved or to love others. In fact, this desire says much about our nature as relational creatures. Nevertheless, the problem comes when love is manipulated or perverted towards selfish ends. True love wants only good for another, whether the one who loves gets loved back or not. The second root, therefore, is the corruption of the search for love and one's place within society; it is *the belief one needs the praise, attention, and even worship from others to be validated.* This is when someone seeks to find their self-worth and dignity from how others perceive them, and not from the inherent value they have from being dignified human persons. Often, it amounts to wanting riches and lavished living because these material things are used to represent one's value and worth, which then leads to others being impressed, which then makes such a person feel better about him or herself. It also feeds off the first root because more possessions serve to increase comfort and thus decrease suffering. Like the first root, this one also has innumerable examples and degrees of severity; at its worse, some are willing to manipulate fellow humans for the purpose of increasing wealth for themselves. For young people, an example of this might be the goal of popularity. Consider how much time, money, and effort goes into attracting members of the opposite sex, or "fitting in" with members of the same sex. The goals to be "hot," "cute," "a pimp," or the almighty, "celebrity" (as opposed to a role model) are all pop-culture examples of seeking to find one's validation and praise from others. The goal of reputation, prestige, or power remains the highest good; the manifestation is the only thing that differs.

> Love is, of course, not merely of the romantic sort. T[o] help you understand differ[]ent types of love, do a we[b] search on the Greek word[s] for love, and write them dow[n] on this chapter's journa[l] pages. Hint: there are fou[r]

But don't I have to love myself and be confident?

The third and final root of slavery's evil is *the belief one can ensure their maximum pleasure and false senses of validation by controlling others.* Compelled by the first two roots, therefore, one seeks to gain power over others to feel greater self-worth, and to have an easier life. This becomes part of the definition of a slave owner; to have power and control over others, again, serves to fuel one's prideful, self-centered, **narcissistic** ideology. Some pop-cultural examples of this might be ethnic or gang-violence including how it is glorified, or the whole "game" aspect to dating where men seek to "play" girls to use them for sex, or when girls seek to gain control over guys by attracting them sexually purely. More extreme cases of this include date-raping and other types of domestic and sexual abuses. Having power in itself is not a bad thing; after all, one of the values of this book is **empowerment**. Having confidence and loving ourselves are not bad either; but we are called to love of ourselves for *what we are,* which is dignified and valuable human persons - not beasts. And because all humans are equally human, this is also how we are to treat others. Enter in the Golden Rule here.

All three of these rotten roots, when embraced completely, are evil. Evil means they are not good according to our nature as humans, and one's embrace of any of them will, in the long run, lead only to emptiness, meaninglessness, boredom, and guilt.

As a dignified person, it is important to avoid these things. You must try always to live life loving people, and not hurting them. Try always to put yourself into other people's shoes.

You have a choice that must be made every day. Choose good. With every passing day, grow less and less guilty of objectifying and using others for your own selfish pleasure or to fill your own desires. Instead, seek to live a life of peace, self-honesty, self-examination, and love. This is not an easy path; it is a path that requires difficult choices and constant awareness of your thoughts and actions. However, only by choosing this path will you begin to live an exciting existence, full of meaning, hope, clarity, and truth.

"Hatred paralyzes life; love releases it. Hatred confuses life; love harmonizes it. Hatred darkens life; love illuminates it."
—Dr. Martin Luther King, Jr.

Case Study: Hitler

Adolf Hitler was responsible for murdering and enslaving millions of people. But did he think what he was doing was wrong? Some say that because of his beliefs about the world and the human race, Hitler thought he was doing a good thing by killing off what he thought to be the weaker people. Not only did he believe in his mind there is such a thing as a "supreme race," Hitler also acted on his convictions; this is why he is a great example of how badly things turn out when one becomes enslaved to crazy false beliefs.

Consider this philosophical first principle: All truth-claims inherently assert their opposing views to be false. For example, if a person says "I believe one plus two equals three" they necessarily claim it does not equal four, five, or six. The same is true for all beliefs because they, by nature, are true or false - never both at the same time. In that light, here is a method that can help guide you in the lifestyle of self-examination:

1. *Pinpoint any held belief. For example, "I believe popularity is important," "I believe freedom is a human right," or deeper ones like, "I believe all is one," "I believe God does (or does not) exist," "I believe humans evolved from early primates," or "I believe truth is relative."*

2. *Define the terms used. Following the examples above, write down*

Question #4

What are some ways mental slavery can take place? Circle all that apply.

A) Ingrained in culture so that the majority of people don't even realize they're enslaved.

B) Long-lasting verbal abuse and brainwashing.

C) Having an addiction to drugs, alcohol, sex, or shopping.

D) It is not possible for people other than 'real slaves' to be mentally enslaved.

E) Other:

what you mean by "popular," "freedom," "God," "all," or "relative."

This is important because if we cannot define the terms of our beliefs, then how can we assess if we really believe these things, let alone determine them to be meaningful or not?

3. Identify any assumptions you've made, and provide justification for your beliefs the best you can. Offer reasons for why you believe what you do and seek to prove your beliefs correct, or ditch them if they're not! Go as deep as you can. When you answer one question then ask "why" to that answer, and so on and so forth. The deeper you get into your foundational beliefs the better. This takes time.

4. Ask yourself, where is the evidence for this belief? Is there a universal law that supports it? Where is the logic for my belief? Does this belief help me or hurt me in life? Does it contradict itself? Is it objectively meaningful? Is it based upon unexamined assumptions about the reality of things?

5. Then, present your beliefs and justifications to smart and insightful people who can challenge you, such as parents, teachers, and well-read peers. Make sure to ask more than one person! Just as important, be sure to read a variety of books with arguments both for and against the belief. By doing so, ideas you may not have considered are sure to arise. These people and books may be right or wrong, but either way you will be given challenges that move you to think and respond. Most importantly, you must allow for the truth to reign. Truth is not determined by what most people say, how people say it, or because of who says it; truth requires some time and energy to discern.

6. You will be forced to improve your understanding and gain clarity, or, in the case your belief is proven untrue, you will be freed from your false belief, and therefore grow in understanding and consistency with the truth. This process makes for an examined life, which is the kind of life you should actively seek.

So, for example:

1. I believe square-circles can be found on the moon.

2. This means, I believe that on the moon there exists a shape that fits the definition of a square and fits the definition of a circle at the exact same time in the exact same respects.

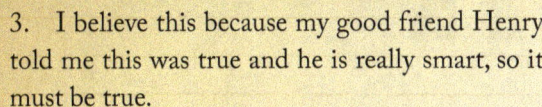

3. I believe this because my good friend Henry told me this was true and he is really smart, so it must be true.

4. There really is no evidence for my belief; in fact, it is a bit weird, now that I think of it. The whole concept of square-circles makes little logical sense.

5. Now, after reading some good philosophy books and presenting this to my teacher who has a college degree in geometry, she suggests my belief is irrational because there is no proof of this, and in fact a square-circle is a rational impossibility. A square, by definition, has four equal straight sides and four equal corners, while a circle has no corners at all. In other words, a square and a circle are nearly opposites, and to say a square-circle is even possible, let alone be found on the moon, is a strict contradiction and violates the second law of thought (see Appendix II). So, there may be squares on the moon and there may be circles on the moon, but it is not rationally possible to say there are square-circles on the moon. This is great since my mind can't even begin to imagine what one would look like either.

6. After talking with my teacher and doing more research, it turns out Henry was lying to me and so now I no longer believe that there are square circles living on the moon. Sweet.

Question #5

Imagine a genie came to you and offered you a slave to do all your schoolwork and no one would ever find out. Honestly, what would best describe your response?

A) You would say no in a split second

B) You would say yes right away

C) You would say yes after one minute of thinking about it

D) You would be tempted but say no

E) Other:

Looking at slavery and the many aspects of it, we can arrange each person's core on a spectrum, where at one end there is slavery and at the other end there is freedom. Every one of us occupies a place in that spectrum based on our behavior and our beliefs; some closer to one end, some closer to the other.

See the illustration below and try to figure out where the following would fit on the spectrum:

- I help out at a soup kitchen
- The King and his descendants have a birthright to the throne; no elections are needed.
- If I were thinner, I would be lastingly happy.
- Humans are equal.
- I am able to prove humans are equal.
- It is clear to me there is no clear truth.
- I spend all my money things that get me the attention I need to feel valuable.
- I love myself, my neighbor, and I live each day to the fullest.
- It is true because I feel so strongly and that's all that matters!

SLAVERY ◄ TYRANNY ◄ DOGMA ◄ FALSE BELIEFS ◄ MEANING ► TRUTH ► KNOWLEDGE ► APPLICATION ► FREEDOM

THINK TANK

Human Dignity

A basic question for us to ask is this: Is there a **moral law**, which slavery violates? In other words, is it clear that humans are equal and have inherent worth, thus making us each responsible to treat all humans with dignity? Philosopher Dr. Owen Anderson addressed the question of clarity and responsibility this way: "What is clear is clear to reason and is, therefore, objectively clear, as opposed to being personally/subjectively clear. The best way to define 'clarity' is to give an example: it is clear that 'a' is not 'non-a.' This is maximal clarity, which is necessary for maximal responsibility." Philosopher Surrendra Gangadean in his book Philosophical Foundation agrees with this and goes a step further when he says, "One does not have to actually know [what is clear] in order to be responsible; it is sufficient that one could know if one wanted to." As it relates to our conversation, this means humans cannot be held maximally responsible to affirm human dignity if it is not maximally and objectively clear that we are responsible to do so. Thus, the study of ethics, as well as **epistemology** and **metaphysics**, becomes critical as the demand to show what is clear presses on us all. To help bring forth clarity, we can start by defining dignity.

Dignity refers to the honor, value, and respect that all living things deserve. The dignity that is to be given to all living things depends on their nature. For example, the nature of a tree is different than the nature of a cat, so we can say they are valuable for different reasons. Further, what is good for something is based on its nature. For example, what is good for a fish is based on the nature of a fish. This is why we can say it's good for them to be swimming in water; it's in line with their nature.

Well, the same is true for humans: what is good for a human is based on the nature of a human. We will discuss this more in the chapters to come, but human beings most basically are **rational** beings. That is, we are all creatures equipped with the ability and potential to use our mind, operated by **reason**. We are all much more than this, of course, but the potential to be rational through the use of reason is the most basic quality to our existence, and is in fact the essential concept to defining a human being in contrast to any other creature. To illustrate consider this: We might talk about people in China, Kenya, Mexico, or in Canada and while these cultures are different, the fact they are all "people" reveals they have the same rational nature as all humans, just like the rest of us.

Modern Philosopher Surrendra Gangadean again says something similar in his book Philosophical Foundation: "There is not a Greek and a non-Greek rationality; there is not a male and a female rationality; there is not an old and a young, or a rich and a poor rationality, although these have become lines of division among human beings. Reason, as the laws of thought in us, is the common ground for all who think."

This means that what is good for any and all of us humans is to use our reason to the fullest; to seek to understand, discover the meaning of life, and to gain knowledge about ourselves, our world including its origin, and our destiny, from which we can find lasting happiness and joy.

It also points out something else very important: There is only one human nature. There is not "slave human nature" and "free human nature." Despite our many differences, we are at the basic level equally human. Therefore, the dignity and value due to any person must be attributed to all people, not just some. If we affirm the human dignity of all people, then rationally, no human can rightfully be property of another.

Consider also what Thomas Jefferson once said: "The world is indebted for all triumphs which have been gained by reason and humanity over error and oppression." This is what you should focus on—using reason to overcome today's unreasonable errors and injustice.

Reason in its fullness is the single, most basic and most important element of this book. This issue will not be dissected in greater detail to avoid getting off the human trafficking topic; however, every exercise and feature in this book appeals to your rational nature. You are encouraged and invited to deepen your studies on the subject of reason.

Now, let's put on our thinking caps! Locate at least one new resource that discusses human dignity. It can be a book, something from the Internet, or a person you talk to, but you should write down what it is and where you found it. Reflecting on the topic, finish by writing a paragraph on the resource you found. If you are not sure what to look for consider searching, "The Age of Enlightenment."

Human Rights

Go to the Web and find Youth For Human Rights' website (youthforhumanrights.org). Spend a half hour or so checking out their site, watch at least two of their videos, and then write down what you find and what you think about it

What was talked about? Do you agree? Disagree? What is said or pointed to concerning human equality? And last, as tied to this Chapter's Think Tank, do we have equal rights if we, as humans, are not equal? Go.

For more, consider also finding, "Pope Peace Depends on Human Dignity" on-line and watching that. It is short but sweet.

Memoirs of a Young Hero

Be true to yourself, be honest, and write out a few paragraphs. By the end of this book these chapter sections will become the personal and unique story of your journey this far.

Having read through this chapter take some time to write down how what you learned makes you feel and the most important thing you will take with you. Then circle on a scale of 1 to 10 the number that best describes how well you affirm the human dignity of others and your own, as described in this chapter's Think Tank.

1   2   3   4   5   6   7   8   9   10

Why is this your answer and how do you feel about it? What are some things you can do to move up a few spots? Also, make note of any important "aha" moments you had while going through this chapter.

Journal Lines

ANSWERS: 1) D 2) True 3) personal 4) A, B & C 5) Personal

THROUGH THE TREES
(A LOOK AT THE HISTORY OF SLAVERY)

CHAPTER 2

Lord Mansfield

"Once an individual's search for meaning is successful, it not only renders him happy but also gives him the capability to cope with suffering."
— Victor Frankl

Slavery is not a new invention. It has been around for a very long time and has taken on many different forms. However, despite these different looks, the root remains the same. Across countries, slavery has been legal and illegal; while some have fought it, others embraced it. In many situations, entire countries proudly and happily used slaves. A very common way slaves were made was through war: after battle, those who won the war forced those who lost into slavery. It was one of their rewards for winning. Nevertheless, in all of its forms slavery is a fundamental denial of human dignity, which is its main problem.

Behind every reality lies an idea. For example, the *reality* of getting up and going to school comes out of the *idea* that education is important. This goes to show some ideas are good. On the other hand, some ideas also can be quite bad. Author Kevin Bales, who wrote the book *Disposable People*, points out how the idea of slavery has been upheld: "I investigated local slavery. In each case I looked hard into how slavery works like a *business*, and how the surrounding community protected slavery *by custom* or *ignored* it in fear." This should suggest to you that all ideas ought to be tested to see if they are true or not. We all ought to examine our lives and customs to see if the things we ignore are keeping slavery alive.

According to historian Milton Meltzer, there are numerous occasions throughout history where slaves rose up and revolted against their oppressors. However, once they had the upper hand of power, instead of continuing to fight for justice and human freedom, they turned around and enslaved the very people who enslaved them. In other words, for whatever reasons they had, it seems their issues was not with slavery itself being an unjust system; it was the fact *they* were the ones being enslaved. This offers a good deal of insight into how cycles of injustice are continued. It also clarifies how slavery is fundamentally an intellectual problem, which needs to be solved first, if the reality of it will ever be stopped.

Question #1

Slavery is merely one way to deny human dignity; what are some other ways denying human dignity can be expressed? Circle all that apply:

A) Focusing on race more than basic human nature

B) Focusing on gender more than basic human nature

C) Seeking material wealth above the wealth of wisdom

D) Treating others as objects for our own pleasure

E) Seeking power through force or lying to the public

F) All of the above

Case Study: Aristotle

Aristotle was a **philosopher** who lived in ancient Greece around 2500 years ago. He provided the world with a tremendous amount of valuable information, in areas such as politics, reason, physics, and even poetry. For instance, Aristotle was a big supporter for living the examined life; however, at the time he lived, slavery was a normal part of life, and he had much to say about it. Clearly some of his ideas on other subjects were good and lived on, since we are talking about him today. Unfortunately, not all of what he argued for was beneficial to us as humans. Check out these quotations that reveal what Aristotle thought about slavery:

"It is manifest therefore that there are cases of people of whom some are freemen and the others slaves by nature, and for these slavery is an institution both expedient and just."
    - Aristotle, *Politics I255a1-2*

"One who is a human being belonging by nature not to himself but to another is by nature a slave; and if a person is a human being belonging to another human being he is an article of property, and an article of property is an instrument for action separable from its owner."
    - Aristotle, *Politics I254a4-18 (Politics I254a4-18)*

"For that some should rule and others be ruled is a thing not only necessary, but expedient; for from the hour of their birth, some are marked out for subjection, others for rule."
    - Aristotle, *Politics I.5*

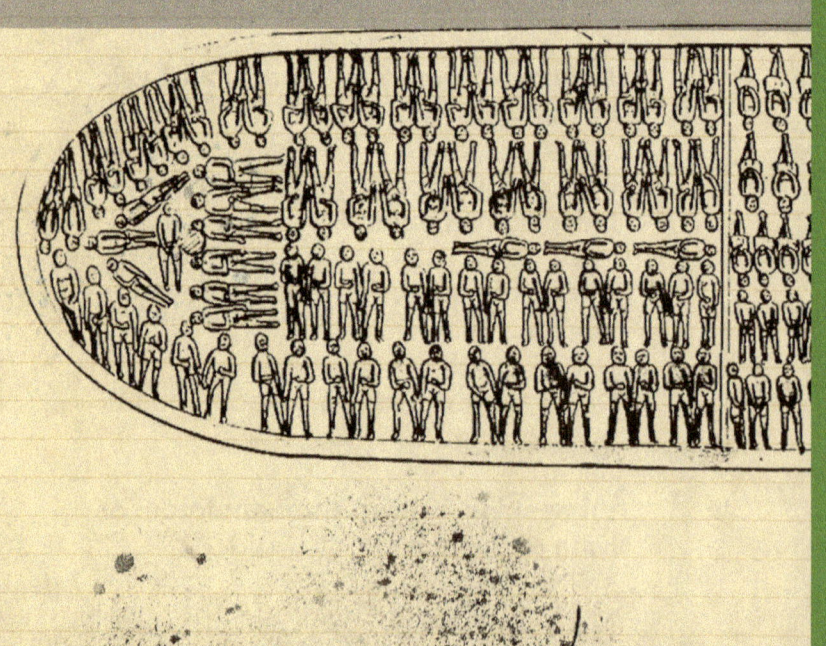

Question #2

Which of the following helped abolish slavery in the United States?

A) War

B) Political debates

C) New social values

D) Philosophical and religious debates

E) Some agreement on basic ideas about human nature

F) All of the above

Aristotle questioned many of the norms in his **culture**; even after examining slavery, however, he still concluded it to be reasonable. He believed some men and women were by nature slaves due to a characteristic some races would have called "servility." In his logic, a country presenting less "spirit" than another country should be naturally enslaved. Not just that, but as historian and author Peter Garnsey noted, "Aristotle considered it important to show, not just that slavery was rooted in nature, but also that there existed a class of people who were naturally fitted to be slaves."

As rational human beings, we know that merely stating Aristotle was wrong is not enough to prove him wrong. Let's try to use reason critically instead:

Aristotle referred to both free men and slave men as "men." This must mean they each had in common the same nature as "men," right? So, here is an example of how a belief can be broken down and, in this case, shown false:

1. All people are human, as Aristotle admitted.

2. What is good for one human according to his or her nature must be good for all humans who share the same nature.

3. Using reason is good for all, since using it is part of our human nature.

4. Using reason requires freedom.

5. Therefore having freedom is good for all people.

6. **Conclusion: Because all humans are human and all need freedom, all humans should be free and should allow others to be free as well.**

A History of Violence

Slavery in Early Mesopotamia

Some 6,000–7,000 years ago, a group of people called Sumerians lived in the area now known as Iraq. These people had two classes: free men and slaves. For the most part, these slaves were captured during wars; the victor realized that putting them to work was more profitable than killing them or placing them in jails. From there, their civilization became more dependent on slaves.

Slavery in Ancient Egypt

Slavery existed in Egypt as early as 4,000 BC. It is speculated that among the thousands of workers it took to build the great pyramids, many were slaves. These slaves are believed to have been mostly foreigners and prisoners of war.

Slavery in Ancient Greece

It's likely that every household in ancient Greece had at least one slave. As we read from Aristotle, slavery in ancient Greece was endorsed by their philosophical and religious worldviews. They taught that some people were born free and some were born as slaves; the real reason Greeks saw slavery as necessary was probably of economic nature. As Greeks conquered more and more cities, they gathered even more slaves who helped their economy boom, and this led to a full-blown legalized slave trade. It's estimated that around 430 B.C. they may have had up to 150,000 slaves in the city of Attica alone; if accurate, this figure would make up close to one third of the whole population. As the Roman Empire grew more powerful, the Greek Empire eventually collapsed.

Slavery in The Roman Empire

In his *Ideas on Slavery*, Peter Garnsey wrote: "The Romans were a practical people. They could see the **integration** within their community of conquered peoples, whether slaves or free subjects, was a recipe for growth and the consolidation of conquest." Consequently, hundreds of thousands of people of all different races and religions suffered enslavement. For example, on the first Jewish-Roman war Romans took a total of 97,000 Jews and sold them into slavery. At some point, the number of slaves in Rome was nearly half of the whole population, which was well into the millions by the end of the second century A.D.

One of the most gruesome ways slaves were used in Rome was to fight in arenas as gladiators. Trained and given weapons, they had to fight elephants, lions, and fellow humans to the death. Thousands of people came to watch in support of such "sport." The Coliseum, Rome's most famous ancient amphitheater, could hold 50,000 people, and when it came time to see bloody battles it could easily be packed full. Through time, attitudes in Rome shifted, slave laws evolved, some slaves were freed, and after the Empire weakened from within, it was eventually conquered.

Question #3

How did Ancient Greece determine the difference between slaves and free people?

A) Race
B) Gender
C) Age
D) Beliefs about human nature
E) None of the above

The Trans-Atlantic Slave Trade

Beginning in the year 1441, the European Slave trade started as a Portuguese sea captain brought 12 Africans as a gift for Prince Henry in Lisbon, Portugal. Numerous people, including the Pope, were on board to begin harvesting slaves. Though many types of people were enslaved, Africans were targeted because of their physical strength, size, and because the continent was close by. It is worth noting that slavery existed within Africa prior to this time; in fact, African tribes sold members of opposing tribes to the Portuguese themselves. Europeans often traded things like glass, beads, whiskey, ivory, and guns in exchange for slaves. Within 11 years, Lisbon's slave population grew to 10,000, which was one-tenth of the country's population. Getting slaves from Africa to the United States, to the Caribbean, or to South or Central America took about 40 days in large ships. Sometimes between 400 and 500 people were chained and stacked up like lumber, where at least 13 out of every 100 died in route. By the 1800s, the slave traders could make well over $30,000 profit per trip—equal to $600,000 in today's terms!

Question #4

Are there any classifications of people (ethnic, religious, nationality) who have not been guilty of slavery at least once through history?

Yes   No

If yes, who?

Slavery in the United States

Slavery existed among the Native Americans when Christopher Columbus and friends first arrived. Then more Europeans came over, and slowly took more and more territory from the natives. Native Americans were initially used as slaves in great numbers, but soon African slaves were preferred, as they were easier to purchase and to control. Once out of Africa, they were at the mercy of their captors; this was not the case with Native Americans who knew the land well. In a **free market** system, where free people could buy and sell goods freely, the demand for slavery in the U.S. increased as the European demand for things like sugar, coffee, cotton, and tobacco increased. Slavery in the U.S. was formally abolished in 1865.

Slavery after the United States

Many think slavery ended after the U.S. abolished it. This is not true. In fact, it continued most everywhere else. In the U.S., slavery was originally about production and not about race, but it grew to be about race because of the obvious distinction of skin color between Africans and Europeans of that era. This, however, was not always the norm in other places. For example, in the mid to late 1800's tens of thousands of Europeans were enslaved by the Turks, which included more than 30,000 Christian slaves in the city of Tunis alone.

What's the Point?

1) Slavery has gone on everywhere and has involved every type of person.

2) Slavery is fueled by so-called economic demands. (You will read about this in Chapter 7 and there is much more in the full version of this book as well.)

3) Slavery has little to do with color, race, or religion. The most vulnerable people have always been targeted to be slaves; however, racial, ethnic, or religious arguments may have been used to justify slavery in the face of its obvious hypocrisy.

4) Slavery can operate in a variety of ways. In many cases, such as in ancient Greece, slaves were allowed a lot of freedom and rights, while in others cases they were completely and entirely abused.

5) Slavery was often a social *norm* that went unquestioned by many. It was a day-to-day reality, where slaves commonly worked in and around the house, in the fields, in the construction of buildings, and in mines, among other places. To them, this was normal and "just the way it is." This should serve as a warning: all of us have norms that haven't been questioned yet, so can we really sleep at night assured our norms are acceptable? Think about how often you say in some form or another, "Everyone does it." This is exactly what many slave owners have said to help them sleep at night, and it might be true—but it is not an excuse.

As you see, attitudes about slavery reflect beliefs about human nature. False views of human nature allows for humans to be mistreated, which leads only to confusion, division, death, war, and slavery.

Question #5

Go to Wikipedia.org and search for their "Abolitionism" page. Read through it, particularly the first portion and the one titled "In The Americas," and write a paragraph about what you learned including the definition of abolitionism and some details on an abolitionist mentioned in the text.

THINK TANK

Happiness

Influenced by philosopher John Locke and others, the United States Declaration of Independence, primarily penned by Thomas Jefferson, says that all men have the right to life, liberty, and the pursuit of happiness. Similarly, many doctors and psychologists say being happy is critical to being healthy. Happiness is a great thing! What makes you happy? Make a list of the top-five things below.

Now, in groups, dig a bit deeper: What is happiness? Is it something that people can just sit down and achieve? As you probably already know, happiness is achieved by action; by reaching what one thinks is good. You must do something to produce happiness. Holocaust survivor Viktor Frankl in his book *Man's Search For Meaning*, recognized this when he said, "As seen, a human being is not one in pursuit of happiness but rather in search for a reason to become happy."

But herein lies the problem: What some people want actually hurts themselves and/or others, even though it produces short-lived happiness. Slave owners were happy because they had others to do their work for them. They were getting what they wanted—leisure, prestige, and power! This raises a good question: Do the things we want truly bring us long-lasting happiness? It is easy to say "I want this" or "I want that," but it is a whole different issue whether or not we *should* really want this or that. When one finds a truly meaningful life, it produces a far greater sense of happiness than any drug or toy could. What do you want out of life? What do you feel you should want? How do your answers differ from your friends, or how are they the same?

Happiness is the result of living a meaningful life based on what is true and good not only for you, but for all living things. We cannot be sure if what we value is good for us without examining our values and the beliefs that support them. So, finding lasting happiness begins by questioning what makes you happy, and discerning whether it is lasting or not.

All of us have something we do that makes us happy. If you like to draw, paint, bake, hike, tinker, dance, communicate with others, or play music then embrace this constructive love and appreciate it on others as well. The examined life means enjoying even the smallest and most simple aspects of goodness, truth, and beauty as we find it in our world, lives, families, and communities. As a wise person once said, don't forget to stop and smell the roses!

Now, let's put on our thinking caps! Locate at least one new resource that discusses happiness. It can be a book, a song, something from the Internet, or a person you talk to, but you should write down what it is and where you found it. Reflecting on the topic, finish by writing a paragraph on the resource you found.

Creation Tank

The History of Slavery in America

Go to an online search engine and do a video search for "The History of Slavery in America videos" — there are three parts. After watching all three parts write at least five sentences of what you learned, what you felt, and tie it to at least one thing you read in this chapter of this book.

Memoirs of a Young Hero:

Be true to yourself, be honest, and write out a few paragraphs. By the end of this book these chapter sections will become the personal and unique story of your journey this far.

Having read through this chapter, take some time to write down how what you learned makes you feel and the most important thing you will take with you. Then circle on a scale of 1 to 10 the number that best describes how happy a person you are as described in this chapter's Think Tank. Keep in mind, not being happy is not in itself a bad thing. Often, we can find ourselves in seasons where happiness is not easily found; the trick is to never stop searching for it.

1   2   3   4   5   6   7   8   9   10

Why is this your answer and how do you feel about it? What are some things you can do to move up a few spots? Also, make note of any important "aha" moments you had while going through this chapter.

Journal Lines

Answers: 1)F 2)F 3)D 4)No 5)Personal

CHAPTER 3

IT'S NOT YOU, IT'S ME
(A NEW KIND OF SLAVERY)

"I am naturally anti-slavery. If slavery is not wrong, nothing is wrong..."
— Abraham Lincoln

Castro Alves

This chapter is a little different from the previous ones. Up to now, you have read about slavery in general and how it has looked throughout history; this chapter will show you how real and present slavery still is today. Many people believe slavery is no longer around; that after it became illegal all across the world, no one else continued to suffer its immoral degradation. It would be wonderful if that were the case, but it is not. In fact, despite being illegal around the world, more slaves exist in the world today than ever before, which is why it is important to correct the common misinterpretation

Question #1
The roots of slavery remain the same despite its different looks throughout history.

    True   False

If you answer "True," what are these roots? If "False," give your reasons.

Question #2

Because slave traders claim humans other than themselves have little value, this makes slavery okay.

True   False

If you answer "False," what value do humans have? If "True," give your reasons:

Modern-day Slavery

Slaves today are cheaper than they've ever been. One hundred and fifty years ago in Mississippi a slave would cost you about $40,000–$100,000 (in today's dollars), depending on how healthy, young, or specialized they were. This caused them to be treated as an expensive piece of equipment. Although without their human dignity affirmed, once purchased they were kept healthy and well-fed, just as you would oil and fuel a car. For the slave-owners, slaves were an investment, and it was to the slave-owner's benefit to keep the slave alive and healthy as long as possible.

But today, it is reported that a person can be bought in India for as little as $90. If a car cost only $90, you probably would not worry about oiling it, or even fueling it for that matter—fuel would end up costing more than a new car. What do you think this means to a modern-day slave?

Today, slaves are typically held for a very short period of time because there are so many vulnerable humans available to be enslaved, which makes it easy to discard them as disposable. This means they are either constantly re-sold to new buyers or killed off. As noted above, one of the biggest components of modern-day slavery is how global it is as there are no limits to where humans are trafficked. In every known country, humans can be bought and sold, making it nearly impossible to stop traffic; they can even be bought and sold on the Internet.

of history, which makes most people believe that slavery has come to an end. The fact is, slavery has never left; it has only changed the way it looks and operates.

This new form of slavery is usually referred to as "modern-day slavery." What is most unique about modern-day slavery is the process used, called human trafficking. Perhaps you've heard of "drug trafficking," which refers to the underground system of harvesting drugs and sneaking them into countries to be sold; well, human trafficking is almost exactly the same, but instead of drugs, the trafficking system hides and sneaks human beings around for the purpose of selling and exploiting them. This is the process by which modern-day slavery operates.

The biggest difference of modern-day slavery from times past is the context in which it exists. The next big difference of today's context is globalization, which will be discussed shortly.

As always, good studies begin with defining basic terms. Following are three of the most important definitions you need to know in moving forward.

Question #3

What is the proper order for changing the world? From one to five, write what you think should come first, second, and so on.

__ Change the whole world

__ Change your values where necessary

__ Change your world-view, i.e., basic beliefs about human nature

__ Change your community

__ Network with others who share the common goal

Hu·man Traf·fick·ing
As defined by the United Nations

(The means for making modern-day slaves)

What it is The recruitment, transportation, transferring, harboring or receipt of persons.

By means of the threat of use of force, coercion, abduction, fraud, deception, abuse of power or vulnerability, or giving payments or benefits to a person in control of the victim.

For the purposes of exploitation, which includes exploiting the prostitution of others, sexual exploitation, forced labor, slavery or similar practices, and the removal of organs.
Consent of the victim is irrelevant where illicit means are established, but criminal law defenses are preserved.

In the past, often endorsed and upheld by governments, slaves were bought, sold, and kept. Because slaves usually came from places far away, and technology was limited, it was harder to transport them. Thus, the demand for slaves was high while the supply was low. Today, however, there are many humans available to enslave. Children are targeted most heavily because they can be transported more easily than adults.

Human trafficking researcher and author David Batstone reported in his book *Not For Sale*, "Human slavery … is not only a serious crisis in China, Thailand, Nepal, Ukraine, and other poor nations. Strong trafficking networks operate covertly within U.S. borders as well and even reach to massage parlors within a few blocks of the White House." This method of hiding in plain sight is one of the things that make ending slavery even more difficult.

Old Slavery
Legal ownership asserted
High purchase cost
Lower profits
Shortage of potential slaves
Long-term relationship
Slaves maintained
Ethnic differences important

Modern-day Slavery
Legal ownership avoided
Very low purchase cost
Very high profits
Surplus of potential slaves
Short-term relationship
Slaves are disposable
Ethnic differences not important

K. Bales (1999) *Disposable People*, California Press

Question #4
Human trafficking is a problem that concerns only those who are affected by it.

True   False

Why or why not?

Glob·al·i·za·tion

Globalization refers to the uniqueness of today's world in contrast to times' past. It is the process of blending by which all the people of the world are unified into a single society and function together. It combines cultural and political forces, including the integration of national economies into the international economy through trade, foreign direct investment, capital flows, migration, and the spread of technology.

Globalization is a term that summarizes three elements:

1) The world is highly *populated*. More than we have known it to be ever before; there are billions of people sharing this planet. The world population has nearly tripled from 2.3 billion to almost 7 billion since 1945. The greatest growth has been in the same areas where slavery is most common today such as Southeast Asia, South America, and India.

2) The *Internet* has greatly increased communication between people who would not be able to communicate otherwise.

3) Due to the invention of the *airplane*, world travel is more accessible today than ever before, which is serving to blend cultures and increase awareness of even the most hard-to-reach places.

These things combined have moved us into what has been called "the age of information," where "**knowledge is power.**" Out of this, international accountability is increased making it harder for evil to be permitted. Sadly, it also is shedding more light on the *conflicts* that exist between nations and cultures, due to incompatible worldviews, values, and social norms.

In plain terms, if anyone asks what globalization is, you might say it means, "The world is getting smaller." In all of this, the central ideas being revealed are: 1) True knowledge of reality is man's greatest good, and 2) all are a part of a global community, equally human and therefore deserve equal treatment. While this has always been the truth, humans have been very spread out throughout the world up to this point, so we have not had to address this issue on such a large scale before.

The current "shrinking" of our world brings us to a big problem: Competing and conflicting views of truth about human nature and human rights. Some nations agree that all humans are equal, and others do not. This happens not because human equality is a **subjective** truth, but instead because these nations fail to acknowledge what is clear to reason. Their behavior is a good example of what neglecting, avoiding, resisting, and denying reason looks like.

Question #5
Talk to a friend about slavery. Start out by asking them if they think it still exists, and then tell them about the things you have been learning. Write a bit here about how your friends react and how the conversation went.

THINK TANK

Invisible Made Visible

Something that's a pretty big deal when talking about human nature is this concept: The invisible becomes visible. No one can ever touch their ideas, personality, thoughts, feelings, or desires because they are invisible. No one can say, "Oh, I see your idea two inches above your head," or something silly like that. Rather, these things are within us, making up what some refer to as the human soul. How, then, are all these invisible things made visible? The mind, emotions, and will, which are the core attributes of the human soul, are expressed through things like words, writing, body language, tone of voice, and the arts.

All that goes on within our mind is made visible when we produce actions out of the choices we make.

As your thoughts establish desires and wants, they move you to make choices, which is where your invisible qualities get revealed in ways that can be seen. Likewise, **virtues** such as courage, **hope**, patience, love—or the lack of virtue, like being dishonest, lustful, or hateful—are all part of your character, which get revealed through your actions. This is why when we examine ourselves to determine what we believe in and value we can just look at our choices and actions, as they will clearly reveal what we hold most dear. Looking at your life choices and actions, what are you revealing about yourself? What are some things you value and believe? If you do not know where to start, look at what you spent your money on in the past few months; this will help you, for better or worse, see some things you value.

Now, let's put on our thinking caps! Locate at least one new resource that discusses the link between ideas and actions. It can be a book, something from the Internet, or a person you talk to, but you should write down what it is and where you found it. Reflecting on the topic, finish by writing a paragraph on the resource you found.

Memoirs of a Young Hero:

Be true to yourself, be honest, and write out a few paragraphs. By the end of this book these chapter sections will become the personal and unique story of your journey this far.

Having read through this chapter, take some time to write down how what you learned makes you feel and the most important thing you will take with you. Then circle on a scale of 1 to 10 the number that best describes how thoughtful you are about the choices you make as described in this chapter's Think Tank.

1   2   3   4   5   6   7   8   9   10

Why is this your answer and how do you feel about it? What are some things you can do to move up a few spots? Also, make note of any important "aha" moments you had while going through this chapter.

Creation Tank

Favorite Songs

Grab a hold of your favorite song and do a web search for its lyrics as well. Now, kick back and listen to it at least once where you won't be distracted. Then listen to it again while reading the lyrics. After doing this, simply journal a bit about why this is your favorite song, how it makes you feel, and discuss what message the lyrics are sending. Lastly, discuss what liking this song might reveal about your values. Feel free to also track down the video if it helps.

Answers: 1) True 2) False 3) 3, 2, 5, 4, then 1 4) False 5) Personal

DEVIL'S IN THE DETAILS
HOW HUMAN TRAFFICKING WORKS

CHAPTER 4

Abraham Lincoln

"The hope which is necessary to endure in the face of what seem like overwhelming odds is not a bare conjectural hope based on mere wish and longing, but a certainty based on understanding the nature of things."

— Surrendra Gangadean

Human trafficking is the process by which modern-day slaves are acquired and sold. It is complex and very hard to track. Below, originally derived by Kevin Bales in his book *Understanding Global Slavery*, are the eight stages human traffickers most often follow to harvest human beings.

Stage One:
Vulnerability

Vulnerability is a key to modern-day slavery. Human traffickers seek victims who can be easily taken advantage of, thus minimizing the chances of getting caught. In general, the most vulnerable people are disadvantaged, lacking basic rights, without education, and above all, in poverty. Traffickers also target women and children, including children who are neglected, abused, or deprived and in need of help. Traffickers seek those who are most in need, who have no one else to help them, and who would be most easily **deceived**.

The reason for this is that it is much easier for traffickers when they have the cooperation of their victims because they will be easier to **manipulate**. This is why the best victims are those who come from disadvantaged places, yet have noble dreams for a better future, education, or employment.

Question #1:
What do those who are most vulnerable need the most? Explain your answer.

A) Basic needs such as food, water, and shelter

B) Opportunities to improve life with medical advancements and good work wages

C) Reformation of cultural norms, values, and beliefs

D) Fellow humans to offer support, resources, and empowerment

E) All of the above

Stage Two: Recruitment

Each situation might differ, but there are many common themes for recruiting slaves. Worldwide, family and community members both knowingly and unknowingly help to recruit slaves, and that is a huge problem. Either they sell the victim to traffickers for a small fee, or parents willingly let their children be taken because they are told they will have a better life, education, or better opportunities.

In other situations, traffickers pose as some type of organization aimed to assist families in finding a better life. Often they entice them with nice clothes or other gifts. Some traffickers will even create an entire fake program pretending to be a model agency or a work-abroad program. In doing this, they hand-pick from several applying people to be sure they get the most suitable slaves. The victims go willingly because they actually think they will have a better life; women may become convinced they will become models, while others may think they will have a chance for a new start in a beautiful, exotic country.

Stage Three: Removal

Removal is when the victim is actually taken from their home into the hands of a recruiter. During this process, the goal for the recruiter is to start taking control of the victim, beginning with mental slavery. In some cases, victims are moved to a collection point where they are brought together with others and prepared for the next stage. Trust is a key element for this stage, and by isolating their victims from their families, the recruiters ensure they are the only ones to be trusted, which makes the next stages go as smoothly as possible.

Stage Four: Transportation

Transporting slaves into different countries can be as easy as putting them in the back of a truck and driving across any given national border. Some countries have tighter border controls, such as the one between the United States and Mexico; still, every year thousands of people get smuggled across the border into the United States, not only from Mexico, but from a number of other countries as well.

To confuse their victims, traffickers will sometimes switch them into many different vehicles, including planes, boats, or trains. Not uncommonly, this includes being drugged and locked in cages, crates, or some other holding cell. Slave traders are cunning and creative; for instance, in 2009 some victims were found trapped in vending machines going across an international border. In this stage, usually the prisoners are moved into various "safe" houses, never staying long in any one place. The goal is to create more confusion and instill fear. After their arrival in a different country, physical abuse typically begins, or simply worsens.

The entire operation is usually extremely organized; there are many different workers doing a number of tasks, and each one specializes in one area only. Like any business, they have supervisors who handle the finances, workers, drivers, and quite often corrupt government workers and police who permit the trafficking to go through their country.

Stage Five: Establishment of Control

If it hasn't already been done, establishing control usually begins with taking away the victims identification (passport, ID cards, or any relevant documents). Many times the traffickers will also obtain photographs of the victims' families back home and threaten to kill everyone if the slave ever tries to run away. **Dependency** on the transporters for everything to survive continues to increase, and victims are still transported from place to place. For children, the manipulation happens much quicker because they are naturally more dependent on adults to meet their basic needs.

Human Trafficking Myths to Know About:
(For more go to: http://nhtrc.polarisproject.org/onlineresources/information-and-resources.html)

1. Trafficking people is not the same as smuggling people, which is when people voluntarily try to sneak into other countries with some help from facilitators. Human smuggling is a crime against national borders, while human trafficking is a crime against people.
2. Trafficking does not require transportation or crossing borders, and does not only happen to immigrants or foreigners.
3. Trafficking does not require physical force or abuse. Psychological abuse based on lies and threats is often used instead.
4. The fact that the victims sometimes have given consent is irrelevant, because they never knew what they were truly giving consent for.

Stage Six: Arrival

Upon arrival to their main destination, the abuse continues to deepen. Here, threats and actual physical or sexual violence are used. As part of their brainwashing and so they won't ask for help, victims are often told that the police are enemies who will throw them in jail. After arrival, they are in a very foreign place, likely unsure of their actual location, and they may not even speak the language. Now both their minds and bodies are ready for the final stage in manipulation, where traffickers transform fellow humans into slaves.

Stage Seven: Exploitation

Exploitation is where victims become full-time slaves: as prostitutes, domestic servants, seamstresses in sweatshops, cotton-pickers on farms, workers for mines, or perhaps simply forced to beg for money. They are forced to work long hours, abusing their bodies, and are given very little food and water. Combining force and violence with mental and often drug abuse, modern-day slaves become very compliant. This makes brainwashing the longest-lasting symptom of all; the victims may no longer question their slavery or look for ways out, and eventually start to think they deserve what they are getting.

> ### Question #2
> Some people argue trafficking victims give permission to be trafficked and thus deserve what they get. On a scale of one to 10 tell us how true you think this is. Then discuss the question with others in your group sharing one another's answers.
>
> 1 2 3 4 5 6 7 8 9 10

Another common tactic is for the victims to be told they're in debt bondage. The victims are told that indeed, they have been brought to a new life and everything will be as promised; but first, they owe the costs of relocation, food, and shelter. They are forced to work to pay back the money with interest. This, of course, never ends, and they become enslaved in the process. More details on this tactic of control are provided in a case study found in the next chapter.

Stage Eight: Resolution

This stage is when the victim's enslavement comes to an end. In many cases, the victim's only way out of slavery is unfortunately through death. Since they are seen as disposable, modern-day slaves are often left to die whenever they can no longer perform the job they were bought to do. If not through sickness (such as HIV/AIDS,) hunger, or murder, a slave may die in a work accident such as untangling fishing nets under water, laboring on construction sites, or dealing with dangerous machines. In some cases victims manage to escape, which of course is a good thing; but they are entirely at the mercy of whoever finds them, and their owner may hurt the slave's family members back home as an act of revenge for the escape. Some are fortunate enough to meet a person or find an organization that is willing to help. Unfortunately, this is far too rare.

Question #3
Having read the eight stages of human trafficking, how do you feel? Circle one and be honest.

   It doesn't affect me

   I'm somewhat affected

   I'm sad

   I'm going to be sick

Question #4
Which of the following are not present in the eight-stage process of human trafficking? Circle all that apply.

   A) Abuse

   B) Deceit

   C) Rape

   D) Benevolence

   E) All of the above

Question #5
How concerned are you about being consistent with the things you claim to believe and the things you do? Explain your answer.

   Very Concerned

   Somewhat concerned

   Not Concerned

THINK TANK

Talents and Hope

As you know, each person has certain natural interests and abilities. These are called *talents*. What people want most out of life will determine what or whom they will serve with their talents. Many times, a talent—such as being a great speaker or being able to sell ice to penguins—can be used to nefarious ends. In reality, the most successful human traffickers have talents and use them to harm other people.

The existence of talents or abilities also reminds us that all humans must work. It cannot be escaped. This does not mean every person has a job, but every person does work; it is part of our nature. Getting up and walking takes work. Reading takes work. "Work" simply refers to the act of putting our body and mind in action towards a desired goal. The easiest work of all comes when we use our natural talents in the course of our work, and the most rewarding work is when we use our talents to bring forth something positive and lasting.

Some say those who dedicate their life to being lazy actually end up working more than other people as it is so contrary to human nature; imagine living in a constant and exhausting act of choosing to not make choices! Further, as the famed psychologist Abraham Maslow once said, "A musician must make music, an artist must paint, a poet must write, if he is to be ultimately at peace with himself. What a man can be, he must be." Though the ways in which they are used might be more or less noble, we all have a drive to use our talents in order to achieve our true potential.

The questions to ask yourself are: What am I working toward? What is my potential, and how will I use it? Where do I put my hope? One thing you should be working toward, as a empowered and dignified person, is to do good toward your fellow humans, and that includes helping to abolish slavery once and for all; ideally, you should use your potential to do this, and many other great things as well. Consider the words of Dr. Martin Luther King, Jr.: "Many people have been plunged into the abyss of emotional fatalism because they did not love themselves properly. So every individual has a responsibility to be concerned about himself enough to discover what he is made for." Surrendra Gangadean goes on to point out in his book *Philosophical Foundation*, "Talent is given to each for all. Talent is not of oneself, by oneself or for oneself. It is for others. There is therefore a moral obligation to serve others through the use of one's talent."

One more thing to keep in mind: No human will work toward something they don't believe can be achieved. This refers to hope. Hopelessness is a bad place to be, because it directly connects to one's meaning in life. If one has no meaning in life, they will also have no hope.

Hope can be true or false. True hope connects with what is actually true about the world and ourselves; false hope is when one has hope in something not founded in truth. For example, if someone has hope in square-circles on the moon, we would say that is a false hope. As for those who work so hard trafficking human beings, they hope the money they find will bring them a meaningful life. They have a false hope, as they will never achieve the satisfaction that comes from having a meaningful life based on using their talents in a positive way, and on a worldview consistent with reality. Like many people before them, they will continue to make negative choices such as power-indulgence, self-infatuation, gluttony, or sloth. Ultimately, these choices lead to meaninglessness and self-destruction, which might seem like a lenient sentence in view of the nature of their crimes, but it is undoubtedly man's greatest possible misery.

At the heart of this Think Tank, then, is the question: Will good overcome evil? Will evil overcome good? Or will they both always exist together forever? What do you believe? Your answer determines where you put your hope and what you work towards. That is, it determines your path in life.

Connecting the dots: We should develop our talents and work toward loving ourselves and others. We must seek and share knowledge. Finally, we should focus on holistically abolishing slavery in the process, with a true hope that it can actually be done. If this does not sell you on developing your talents and reaching your potential, consider what well-respected psychologist Abraham Maslow had to say about it: "If you deliberately plan on being less than you are capable of being, then I warn you that you'll be unhappy for the rest of your life." The choice is yours.

Remember to not make the common mistake of putting your own personal happiness over your fellow humans'. Narcissism and nihilism not only lead to individual self-destruction, but in the societies where these views are embraced by the majority of the population social disunity brews, and from there destruction occurs through anarchy, tyranny, civil war, and/or genocide. We are all equally valuable humans; there is little room to boast, and much room to serve one another.

Now, let's put on our thinking caps! Locate at least one new resource that discusses the importance of developing our talents. It can be a book, something from the Internet, or a person you talk to, but you should write down what it is and where you found it. Reflecting on the topic, finish by writing a paragraph on the resource you found.

 Creation Tank

History of Hip - Hop

Conduct a search on topics such as, "African American Spirituals," "Negro Spirituals,", the history of Jazz, and/or the history of hip-hop. Check out documentaries, websites, and other resources you may know about. Be sure to locate some of the earliest hip-hop artists, listen to them, and jot down what you think about them. Some Hip-Hop songs contain strong language, and so make sure to get your parent's permission before checking some of them out; there are clean versions of many songs available as an alternative. Consider how hip-hip birthed out of other music genres including how it finds its origins in anti-slavery music. Then, answer this question: do you think the current world of hip-hop is being consistent with its roots? Support your argument.

Memoirs of a Young Hero

Be true to yourself, be honest, and write out a few paragraphs. By the end of this book these chapter sections will become the personal and unique story of your journey this far.

Slave owners and human traffickers have talents. However, they use them to abuse others for personal gain. That being said, take some time to write down at least one of your talents and rank how well you have been using it to serve others.

1   2   3   4   5   6   7   8   9   10

Why is this your answer and how do you feel about it? What are some things you can do to move up a few spots? Also, make note of any important "aha" moments you had while going through this chapter.

Answers: 1) C or E 2) Personal 3) Personal 4) A, B & C 5) Personal

LIFE IN FUNHOUSE MIRRORS
(HOW MODERN-DAY SLAVES ARE USED)

CHAPTER 5

Olaudah Equiano

"Noble souls, through dust and heat,
Rise from disaster and defeat
The stronger."
— Henry Wadsworth Longfellow

There is a reason why human traffickers and slave owners are doing all this work of collecting and smuggling people. They traffic people, quite simply, to make a profit, either by putting them to work, or by selling them to someone who will put them to work. In doing so, they usually get really rich—financially, that is.

Former slave Booker T. Washington observes the Catch-22 of violence and oppression when he said, "One man cannot hold another man down in the ditch without remaining in the ditch with him."

For these people, finding the comfort, indulgence, power, and security they seek from material possessions comes at the expense of human lives. They attempt to find meaning through meaningless acts. It's deeply and entirely wrong on many different levels, including for their own personal growth. If they would stop and think introspectively, maybe they'd see life is much more than cars, houses, clothes, big necklaces, or whatever it is they purchase. But most slave-owners apparently do not take the time to analyze their actions, and instead exploit **innocent** people for their own selfish gains. Here are some types of work modern-day slaves endure.

Forced Labor

Forced labor historically is the most common form of slavery. The goal for the slaveholders is to increase production and therefore increase profits. Labor for modern-day slavery is found in four general areas:

- **Fields:** Picking fruits and vegetables, farming and slaughtering animals, harvesting crops of cotton or various grains, and other jobs such as these. Long hours and hard work are typical for this form of slavery.

- **Water:** Various types of fishing, along with swimming in deep cold water to untangle nets, which costs the lives of thousands of children.

- **Factories and Sweatshops:** Building products of any sort such as toys or household goods, sewing clothes in sweatshops, sewing carpet, etc.

- **Domestic Work:** Working as nannies, maids or housekeepers in homes and being forced to clean, cook, endure sexual enslavement, and tend to children. Working in nail salons, restaurants, stores, landscaping, construction, magazine sales crews, or candy sales crews are all common as well. These folks might look like they're working by choice but are in fact unable to leave, suffering beatings, and other such treatment.

Question #1
How much do you think you contribute to human trafficking? Circle all that apply.

A) My clothes might be made by slaves

B) I have contributed to slavery by not knowing much about it

C) My shoes might be made by slaves

D) The food I eat might be grown and gathered by slaves

E) I don't contribute to slavery

Question #2
People who are poor and uneducated deserve what they get when trafficked.

True   False

Explain your answer.

Forced Warfare

Forced warfare is a form of slavery prevalently found in parts of Africa, predominantly Uganda, but also Rwanda, Sierra Leone, Ivory Coast, and other locations. It is estimated that half of the world's children soldiers are located in the African continent. Rebels raid villages kidnapping children, and they use fear as a tool for enslavement. Rebels usually begin the process by killing a few children while others watch. Using drugs, **brainwashing**, violent abuse, and forced military combat with guns and machetes, these children are trained to hurt and murder others. If the brainwashing is totally effective, these kids will forget their former freedoms and truly conform to being violent soldiers. If they don't conform, they themselves will most likely be killed. For more on this go to www.invisiblechildren.com; to find out what other countries in the world use children in their armies, search "Military use of children" on Wikipedia.

Question #3

Regarding illegal drugs, would you say that they are only bad for humans when they are forced to take them? Or are they bad no matter what?

A) All illegal drugs are bad for humans no matter what

B) Some illegal drugs are not bad

C) Drugs are only bad when people are forced or tricked into taking them

D) I am undecided

E) Other:

Forced or Tricked Organ Removal

Organ Removal is one the most mind-blowing uses of human trafficking to date. Here trafficking victims are tricked, convinced, or forced to give up various bodily organs, such as their lungs or kidneys. These organs are then sold on the black market to people who are in need. Most horrifically, this can include victims who are actually killed and pieced apart for their organs to be sold.

Sexual Exploitation

Sexual exploitation comes in many forms. It happens to men, women, boys, and girls of every age.

Brothels: Still legal in many places such as France, Germany and the Netherlands, brothels are essentially houses where prostitutes live together. Locals and travelers visit brothels in order to purchase sex. While it does not happen in every case, the brothel institution makes it easy to keep sex slaves away from their families and previous lives. Brothels are hotbeds for trafficking victims to be kept against their will, typically forced to have sex with well over ten people per day. The prostitution trade also becomes more severe and depraved in some cities, fueling sexual tourism.

Sexual Tourism: A trade that involves "tourists" who purposefully travel to specific destinations to purchase sex. Particularly, sex that is illegal where they come from, such as sex with young children; places such as Thailand, India, Cambodia, Brazil, and Mexico are notorious for offering sex slaves of all ages to a willing and paying customer.

Prostitution: Quite similar to the above, though prostitution is common worldwide and not just in isolated places. Prostitution can be found all throughout Europe, Russia, Asia, Canada, Mexico, South and Central America, the United States, and everywhere in between. Whether it's through online ordering, newspaper ads, boat cruises, or other creative means, trafficking victims can find themselves forced into this trade; they can also be controlled by pimps working on the street, in hotels, or at truck stops. And again, age does not matter; the selling of children of all ages is quite common. In fact, the average age of entry into prostitution is 13.

Pornography: While pornography comes in many shapes and forms, it can also be a product of sex slavery. Quite often sex slavery can include forced pornography where the victims are videotaped or photographed. This way the videos and pictures can be sold as another way to make their holders rich. Child pornography and violent sex acts are a large part of this trade.

Massage Parlors: One way prostitution gets hidden is within "massage" parlors where they claim to only give normal body massages. However, this is not the case, as they also end up providing sexual favors as well. These are most common in places where prostitution is illegal; they are very common in the U.S. and other western countries.

Forced Mail Brides: As strange as it sounds, there is a trade for women to be sold into marriage. This way the slavery looks like a legal arrangement as a man purchases a wife. She is transported to him, and they legally get married. Note there are "mail order brides" who sell themselves into marriage by free will, usually to escape a hard life and/or gain citizenship into a better country. What is being talked about here, however, are those who are forced into it and then find themselves in an oppressive and abusive situation.

Case Study: Debt Bondage

Debt bondage is one of the most common tricks slave holders use to maintain control of trafficking victims. Usually it goes something like this:

1. A person willingly goes with their recruiter, believing they are off to a better life somewhere else. They are promised a good school, or better paying work, or something similar. Sometimes the victim is told that they will become a model or somehow famous.

2. Once they have gone with the recruiter, they then pass through however many other hands to eventually reach their final destination. This is the process talked about in chapter 4.

3. When they reach their final destination they are told that they have amassed a large debt from traveling costs, which they must pay off. To do so, they are then put to work to "pay off their debts." After they do, they will be free and allowed to go to school and work for pay, as they were first told.

4. The hook is that victims are building more debt even as they work, which comes from their food and housing costs, or even for drug habits that they now have because they were at some point drugged by force.

5. So, they already have debt and they are steadily building more. This trick is designed to keep them enslaved for life as they are always working to pay off a never-ending debt.

6. At the heart of this plan is the need to always keep the slave hopeful. Remember, hope is what drives all humans to work. Without hope, no human will work. Like a carrot always dangling in front of a horse's nose, this is where debt bondage then becomes a form of **mental slavery** as well.

7. Lastly, this trick is also used to enslave the children of slaves as the debt passes on through generations. Some kid whose dad was a slave is told he must now work to pay off his father's debt. In India, some families were found who went through three or more generations of being in debt bondage.

Having read this, it is important to see that even regular types of debt, such as credit card debt, can really limit us. Living the examined life, it is highly preferable each of us stays out of needless debt because it can cost us our freedom.

Question #4
Is it possible to give consent for something that causes us harm?

Yes   No

In a group, divide into two different groups to debate the content of this question. One group argues for, "Yes" and the other group argues for, "No." Each group offer reasons for the position and then challenge each other. Do this for at least 15 minutes.

Question #5
Because slavery has gone on for so long, it is something no one will ever be able to stop. True or false?

True   False

Forgiveness

Forgiveness is a critical part of the human experience. If you forgive someone, it is assumed that they did something wrong against you. When this is done, some think they need to disregard the wrong, let it slide, and simply accept the "sorry" or pretend it never happened. This is not forgiveness. True forgiveness admits and acknowledges that wrong was done, allowing the person who was mistreated the chance to say, "What you did hurt, it was wrong, you are responsible, it means something to me, and in that context I choose to forgive you." Forgiveness does not set aside justice; rather, forgiveness comes in light of justice. Justice can and must always be served, however people as individuals can still choose to forgive. We are often in need of forgiveness for wrongs committed, and so it is important to remember to forgive others as we ourselves want to be forgiven.

Forgiveness is defined as letting go of resentment, anger, grudges, and desires for revenge toward the person who has committed harm. It works similarly to forgiving a debt; if someone does their friend wrong in some way, they build an emotional debt, and to make things right they must admitting guilt and whatever else may be necessary in the given situation. Yet, even if the guilty party refuses to make things right, the wronged person may still choose to forgive the debt. One might do this recognizing justice will be served in other ways, as guilt and the accumulated consequences of bad actions will always lead to self-destruction in one form or another.

Some suggest the ongoing struggle in cultures where slavery was once legal happens because forgiveness has not been achieved. Perhaps forgiveness hasn't happened because justice has not been rightly served. For example, in the United States (as in many other countries) where racism and segregation was common, freedom has been given to all, but has there been forgiveness? Did the guilty parties admit and acknowledge their wrongs? If they did, were those who were mistreated accept it, and was justice served? If not, did the victimized parties forgive nonetheless, if for no other reason than to free themselves from the weight of the past?

Forgiveness demonstrates strength, not weakness; it affirms the human dignity and worth of both parties. For the forgiving person, it is a way to keep that wrong from continuing to hurt. Grudges always weigh on the one who holds them, never the one whom they are against. As for the person being forgiven, they can admit they did wrong and accept the forgiveness, or they can harden their hearts and reject it. Either way, the person who forgives is set free of the burden.

Choosing to walk as a humble life-learner, being prepared to give and receive forgiveness, one will quickly get the picture about how much self-examination and self-work it takes to live with integrity. It's not an easy life, but it is a good life. And doing so may be the key for all of us to break away from hating others and move into loving others, which makes a far better world for everyone. It will be good for you to recognize how this conversation fits into the study of Truth and Reconciliation, which deals with ending cycles of violence where it has persisted for generations. For a glimpse of how this could work, consider finding and watching the documentary, Sins of My Father. There are also a lot of eye-opening videos and readings on this topic related to the Rwandan Genocide of 1994, which you should look into. Go to: www.asweforgivemovie.com to get details on a good one. It is available for sale on-line (but check with your local library first).

Now, let's put on our thinking caps! Locate at least one new resource that discusses forgiveness. It can be a book, something from the Internet, or a person you talk to, but you should write down what it is and where you found it. Reflecting on the topic, finish by writing a paragraph on the resource you found.

Creation Tank

Victim Stories

This book does not relay the stories of specific people who have been entrapped in human trafficking. However, there are millions of stories to be told. Do some good research here and find the story of someone who has been trafficked, possibly near where you live. There are countless resources to tap. Try all the human trafficking websites including www.slaverymap.org, or try a web search with "human trafficking" along with the name of your country, state, or city. Today you are the reporter, so do some research and write a brief biography of a person or story you find, followed with your reaction to it.

Memoirs of a Young Hero

Be true to yourself, be honest, and write out a few paragraphs. By the end of this book these chapter sections will become the personal and unique story of your journey this far.

Having read through this chapter take some time to write down how what you learned makes you feel and the most important thing you will take with you. Then circle on a scale of 1 to 10 the number that best describes how easy it is for you to forgive yourself and others as described in this chapter's Think Tank.

    1   2   3   4   5   6   7   8   9   10

Why is this your answer and how do you feel about it? What are some things you can do to move up a few spots? Also, make note of any important "aha" moments you had while going through this chapter.

Journal Lines

Answers: 1) Hopefully E, but probably A, B, C & D   2) False   3) Personal   4) Yes   5) False

CHAPTER 6: NUMBERS ARE LIKE BEARS
(STATISTICS ON HUMAN TRAFFICKING)

William Wilberforce

Whenever dealing with a problem, it is important to first know how big it is. Without understanding how big the problem is, you won't know how big of an effort it will take to solve. Further, good statistics are necessary when talking to government **leaders** because they often just want the facts. When you sit down with political leaders (whether in your township, county, city, state, or nation) to fight for justice, they will be sure to ask how big the problem is specific to the area they work in. How well you can show significance might be the difference between getting support or not.

Sadly, human trafficking is one of the hardest things to get good statistics on. The very nature of human trafficking is underground, unseen, and across borders; one of our biggest needs to abolish human trafficking, therefore, is to get good statistics. This is no small task! It requires uniting people who have different skills, such as computer skills, communication skills, or those who can travel around the world; people who are basically willing to get in the trenches.

Seeing this need for good statistics and proof, top researcher on human trafficking Kevin Bales once said, "There is a part of me that looks forward to being attacked by other researchers for my interpretations, because then a viable field of inquiry will have developed." Notice he welcomes challenges, which as stated before is important in the examined life to help us reach the truth. Kevin Bales also points out, "When we hear about slavery in our midst, the tendency is to think, 'Not in my town.' In a way, we consider ourselves above it, especially if we live in comfortable, relatively trouble-free communities. The harsh truth is, modern-day slavery is in your town."

Though there are not tons of statistics on modern-day slavery, there are some pretty good statistics on poverty and education. Poverty and a lack of education serve to create vulnerability, which increases the likelihood of being trafficked. The more poverty can be decreased and education increased, the quicker modern-day slavery can be abolished.

Question #1

Are you up for the challenge to abolish modern-day slavery?

Yes
No
I will be
I hope so

If yes, what will you do to assist?

"If any man seeks for greatness, let him forget greatness and ask for truth, and he will find both."

– Horace Mann

Statistics on Poverty

(Thank you to www.globalissues.org for compiling the following statistics and making them available)

Poverty generally refers to situations where people find it difficult to meet minimum requirements for an acceptable standard of living of food, water, and shelter. This might be due to a lack of resources, income, education, knowledge, and could be influenced by negligence and/or addictions, but also because of **oppression**, inequality, **tyranny,** or other forms of injustice.

- At least 80 percent of humanity lives on less than $10 per day.
Source: Shaohua Chen and Martin Ravallion, *The developing world is poorer than we thought, but no less successful in the fight against poverty,* **World Bank, August 2008**

- Almost two in three people lack access to clean water and survive on less than $2 a day, with one in three living on less than $1 a day Roughly 25,000 children die each day due to poverty.
Source: 2006 United Nations Human Development Report, pp.6, 7, 35

From UNICEF:

- 2.5 billion people lack access to improved sanitation

- 1 billion children are deprived of one or more services essential to survival and development

- 22 million infants are not protected from diseases by routine immunization

- 8 million children worldwide died before their 5th birthday in 2009

- 4 million newborns worldwide are dying in the first month of life

- 2 million children under 15 are living with HIV

- Nearly 500,000 women die each year from causes related to pregnancy and childbirth

Source: State of the World's Children, 2010, UNICEF, p.18-19

Question #2
The root causes of old slavery and new slavery are the same.

True   False

Why? What are the root causes?

Question #3
Why is it important to have informative statistics on human trafficking?
Circle all that apply.

A)   Because it's nice to know.

B) Because we need to know how big the problem is before being able to take it out.

C)   Because we need to know where in the world the problem exists.

D)   For shock value.

E)   Because we need to know what supports the traffickers.

Education

Education—including reading, writing, and general life skills—is critical for potential victims to avoid enslavement, but above all to have a better life. At its finest, education is the exact process by which individuals learn about their talents and develop them to then serve others. Further, knowledge about human biology, human development, water sanitation, farming, and basic human nature are critically needed in the world's poorest areas to minimize vulnerability of its people and to maximize the area's maturity, independence, and the positive human experience overall.

It is important to point out that trafficking victims do get educated; slaves are educated on how to work in the fields or on how to be prostitutes. So, there is good education and bad education. The question is: Is what we are being taught actually true and good for us? It may well be the case that what appears to be education is merely indoctrination. This is why this book advocates strongly for you to not simply memorize information, but to learn how to use reason critically to derive meaning, truth, and then knowledge from that information. This is a different approach because when you memorize information and casually accept it, you simply assume and believe what is being taught is true; but when you acquires knowledge, you are actually coming to know something is true and can prove it as true.

And that is real power.

Statistics on Education

- **101 million children are not attending primary school, with more girls than boys missing out.** Source: *The State of the World's Children,* 2010, UNICEF, p.18-19

- **Today, nearly one billion people are unable to read a book or sign their names.** Source: *The State of the World's Children,* 1999, UNICEF

- **121 million are out of education altogether.** Source: *The State of the World's Children,* 2005, UNICEF

Statistics on Human Trafficking

27 million – Number of people in modern-day slavery across the world

Source: Kevin Bales, *Free the Slaves*.

According to the U.S. Department of State's 2007 Trafficking in Persons Report (TIP Report), estimates vary from 4 to 27 million.

The International Labor Organization (ILO) estimates 2.4 million people were victims of human trafficking from 1995-2005. This estimate uses the UN Protocol definition of human trafficking, and includes both transnational and internal data.

Slavery has been outlawed in every country but still occurs everywhere

Source: The Universal Declaration of Human Rights, www.un.org/Overview/rights.html

There are more **Slaves in the world today than at any other time in history**

Source: Kevin Bales, *Disposable People: New Slavery in the Global Economy* : 2004

800,000 – Number of people trafficked across international borders every year

Source: U.S. Department of State, *Trafficking in Persons Report*: 2007.

Note: The TIP Report in 2001 and 2002 estimated this figure at 700,000; The TIP Report of 2003 reported 800,000 to 900,000 victims; The TIP Reports of 2004 through 2006 reported 600,000 to 800,000 victims.

32 billion dollars – Total yearly profits generated by the human trafficking industry:

$15.5 billion made in industrialized countries

$9.7 billion made in Asia

Source: ILO, *A global alliance against forced labor*: 2005.

80% - Percent of transnational victims who are women and girls

Source: U.S. Department of State, *Trafficking in Persons Report*: 2007

70% - Percent of female victims who are trafficked into the commercial sex industry

This means that 30% of female victims are victims of forced labor.

Source: U.S. Department of Justice, *Assessment of U.S. Government Activities to Combat Trafficking in Persons*: 2004.

161 - Number of countries identified as affected by human trafficking:

127 countries of origin

98 transit countries

137 destination countries

Source: UN Office on Drugs and Crime, Trafficking in Persons: Global Patterns: April 2006.

Note: Countries may be counted multiple times and categories are not mutually exclusive.

50% - Percent of transnational victims who are children

Source: U.S. Department of Justice, Report to Congress from Attorney General John Ashcroft on U.S. Government Efforts to Combat Trafficking in Persons in Fiscal Year 2003: 2004.

$13,000 - Total amount generated every year on average by each "forced laborer."

This number can be as high as $67,200 per victim per year.

Source: ILO, *A global alliance against forced labor*: 2005.

$80,000 - Average monthly profit of Thailand brothels.

Source: Kevin Bales, *Disposable People*.

Human Trafficking is now considered the 2nd largest and fastest growing illegal trafficking activity in the world

Source: United Nations Office on Drugs and Crime, 2008, www.unodc.org/unodc/en/frontpage/united-nationsgeneral-assembly-urges-stronger-action-against-human-trafficking-.html

Love146, www.love146.org/uploads/the%20bare%20stats_handout.pdf

One Million - Number of children exploited by the global commercial sex trade, every year

Source: U.S. Department of State, *The Facts About Child Sex Tourism*: 2005.

100 to 1500 - Number of clients served per year, per child prostitute

Source: Child Exploitation and Obscenity Section, 2007.

Forced Labor is most prevalent in five sectors of the U.S. economy:

- **46%** in Prostitution and sex services
- **27%** in domestic services
- **10%** in agriculture
- **5%** in sweatshop/factory work
- **4%** in restaurant/hotel work

This number can be as high as $67,200 per victim per year.

Source: David Batstone, *Not for Sale: The Return of the Global Slave Trade-- and How We Can Fight It,* pg. 228: 2007.

Between 100,000 and 300,000 - Number of children in the United States who are at risk for sex trafficking each year

Source: U.S. Department of Justice: Child Exploitation and Obscenity Section, 2007

2.8 million - At least this many children live on the streets, a third of whom are lured into prostitution within 48 hours of leaving home.

Source: U.S. Department of Justice: Child Exploitation and Obscenity Section, 2007

www.usdoj.gov/criminal/ceos/prostitution.html)

"There are more slaves in the world today than at any other time in history."

Question #4

Which of the previous statistics surprises you the most?

A) There are 27 million slaves worldwide

B) Human trafficking brings in an estimated profit of $13 Billion per year

C) At least 14,500 slaves are trafficked into the U.S. each year

D) The average brothel in Thailand profits over $80,000 per month.

E) Other:

Why?

Question #5

Considering there are almost 7 billion people on earth today, which statement is most true?

A) Because there are so many humans no one is really that valuable.

B) The Earth has almost 7 billion extremely valuable humans living on it.

C) It is the jewels, gold, and platinum on Earth that are most valuable.

D) Some people are valuable but not all.

E) Other:

Explain your answer.

Integrity

Integrity is not the same as sincerity. We, as people, can sincerely believe something; however, integrity refers to us acting consistently with what we claim to believe, while at the same time upholding a certain higher ethical code.

It is important to remember that our actions reflect what we believe in. So, if we act in ways that are not consistent with our claimed beliefs, we are not being honest with ourselves about what we really believe in. Having integrity starts with being concerned to live consistently with what we claim to believe in.

Have you ever had a friend who always says he or she will do something but never does it? This is an example of being inconsistent and therefore reveals a lack of integrity. In the United States, the Declaration of Independence says all men are created equal and endowed with the rights to life, liberty, and the pursuit of happiness. As a nation, the United States lacked integrity because it lacked consistency with its claims. Similarly, today slavery is illegal everywhere, but also goes on everywhere. So it may be said that there is a lack of integrity in the world. Deeper still, integrity aims to have **unity** within oneself so that your thoughts, your words, and your actions are in synchrony; a lack of integrity equates a lack of unity. Consider the following fable commonly attributed to Mohandas Gandhi; while it is not possible to verify its accuracy, it personifies Gandhi's concern with integrity:

One day a mother came to Gandhi with her little boy for help. She asked Gandhi, "Please, Bapu, will you tell my little boy to stop eating sugar. He simply eats too much sugar and will not stop."

Gandhi told the mother to leave and come back with the boy in three days.

The mother returned with her son and said to Gandhi, "We have come back as you asked."

Gandhi turned to the boy and said, "Young boy, stop eating sweets. They are not good for you."

The mother then asked Gandhi, "Bapu, why didn't you tell my son that when we first came to see you? Why did you ask us to leave and come back in three days? I don't understand."

Gandhi said to the woman, "I asked you to return with the boy in three days, because three days ago, I, too, was eating sweets. I could not ask him to stop eating sweets so long as I had not stopped eating sweets."

Do you think the whole world can have unity, when the individuals who make up the world lack it? How do you feel when someone who does not obey a certain rule tells you to? Or, have you ever gotten mad at someone for doing something, while you still do it as well?

Personal integrity is a prerequisite for unity; if cultures allow for a lack of integrity there will not be unity, and where there is no unity, there also will be no peace. To illustrate this, think about how important unity is to even life's most simple things. Imagine trying to put your pants on with one arm while the other arm is taking them off. Or, when walking, what if one foot turns left but the other foot goes right? These are funny examples of what your body lacking unity would be like. Putting your pants on can only happen if both your arms are working consistently; also, you cannot turn left and right at the same exact time. In other words, you need to have some degree of unity within yourself just to get dressed and go for a walk. It's no different with any other part of our existence! The point is, if you want unity within yourself, examine all of yourself, and seek to have integrity in all you do. Hold up your moral compass and use it to guide your integrity. Every time you catch yourself lacking integrity, stop and think about why, and make changes.

It should be noted that where one believes foul things or mere falsehoods, even if they are consistent with such beliefs, they are still missing the mark. It would be like saying Hitler had integrity because he acted on his claims and beliefs. While that might seem true, his beliefs were false, cruel, and unethical; so, while he did have consistency, he did not have integrity.

Now, let's put on our thinking caps! Locate at least one new resource that discusses integrity and how it should be cultivated from a young age. It can be a book, something from the Internet, or a person you talk to, but you should write down what it is and where you found it. Reflecting on the topic, finish by writing a paragraph on the resource you found.

Creation Tank

Poverty Cure

Poverty Cure is an organization and DVD series that explores the concept of poverty and how it can be alleviated. They provide a unique voice to the conversation about how to alleviate poverty and best serve others in developing nations and it is worth listening to. Visit povertycure.org and read their, "Vision and Goals," and watch at least three of their video clips found under, "Media." Then, write your thoughts. What surprised you? What are some things you agree or disagree on? What are some things you want to learn more about?

Memoirs of a Young Hero

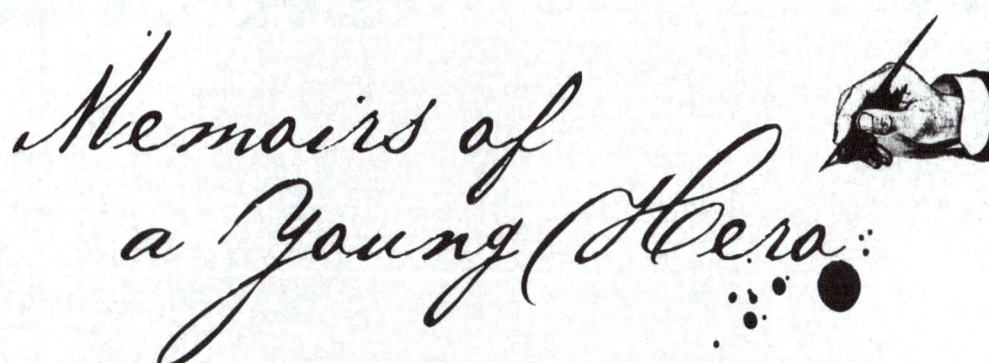

Be true to yourself, be honest, and write out a few paragraphs. By the end of this book these chapter sections will become the personal and unique story of your journey this far.

Having read through this chapter, take some time to write down how what you learned makes you feel and the most important thing you will take with you. Then circle on a scale of 1 to 10 the number that best describes how concerned you are about your personal integrity, as described in this chapter's Think Tank.

1   2   3   4   5   6   7   8   9   10

Why is this your answer and how do you feel about it? What are some things you can do to move up a few spots? Also, make note of any important "aha" moments you had while going through this chapter.

Journal Lines

CHAPTER 7
BECAUSE THE TV SAID SO, DANG!
(A LOOK INTO SUPPLY AND DEMAND)

"Those who prize freedom only for the material benefits it offers have never kept it for long"
— Alexis de Tocqueville

Frederick Douglass

Economy refers to the fiscal wealth and resources of human society. Resources can be not only in the form of products and services derived from natural resources such as water, rock, wood, oil, or soil, but also the human talent, knowledge, ability, and creativity it takes to develop natural resources. Wealth, in the economic sense, refers to the quantity of valuable possessions derived from buying, selling, and trading resources, goods, and services. While there are numerous things that go into accounting the wealth of a nation—early childhood mortality, education, degree of violence, rate of unemployment, per capita income—the easiest way to determine wealth is by how much gross national income a nation makes; in other words, wealth can be measured in money.

Economy, resources, and wealth determine **economic laws** found in and between human societies. They are not evil; they are a natural part of progress. What is evil, however, is when economic laws are obeyed while the more basic moral laws are ignored. This is what slavery does: It reaps the benefits of human talents and work, while ignoring the more basic moral law requirement to affirm human dignity.

Question #1
What best describes how you usually spend money? Circle all that apply.

A. Wants but not necessarily needs

B. Wants and need

C. To create a certain image through things like fashion or add-ons for your car

D. To develop your talents such as taking music lessons, job training, or college preparation

E. Other:

Economics is not bad. Profits are not bad. It is a **natural right** for people to benefit from their own labor. In fact, it is precisely this benefit that can be used to serve others. Profits allow companies to grow, create jobs, and provide products and services we need. Now, check out the chart on the next page to better understand a few of the main economic laws.

Economics 101

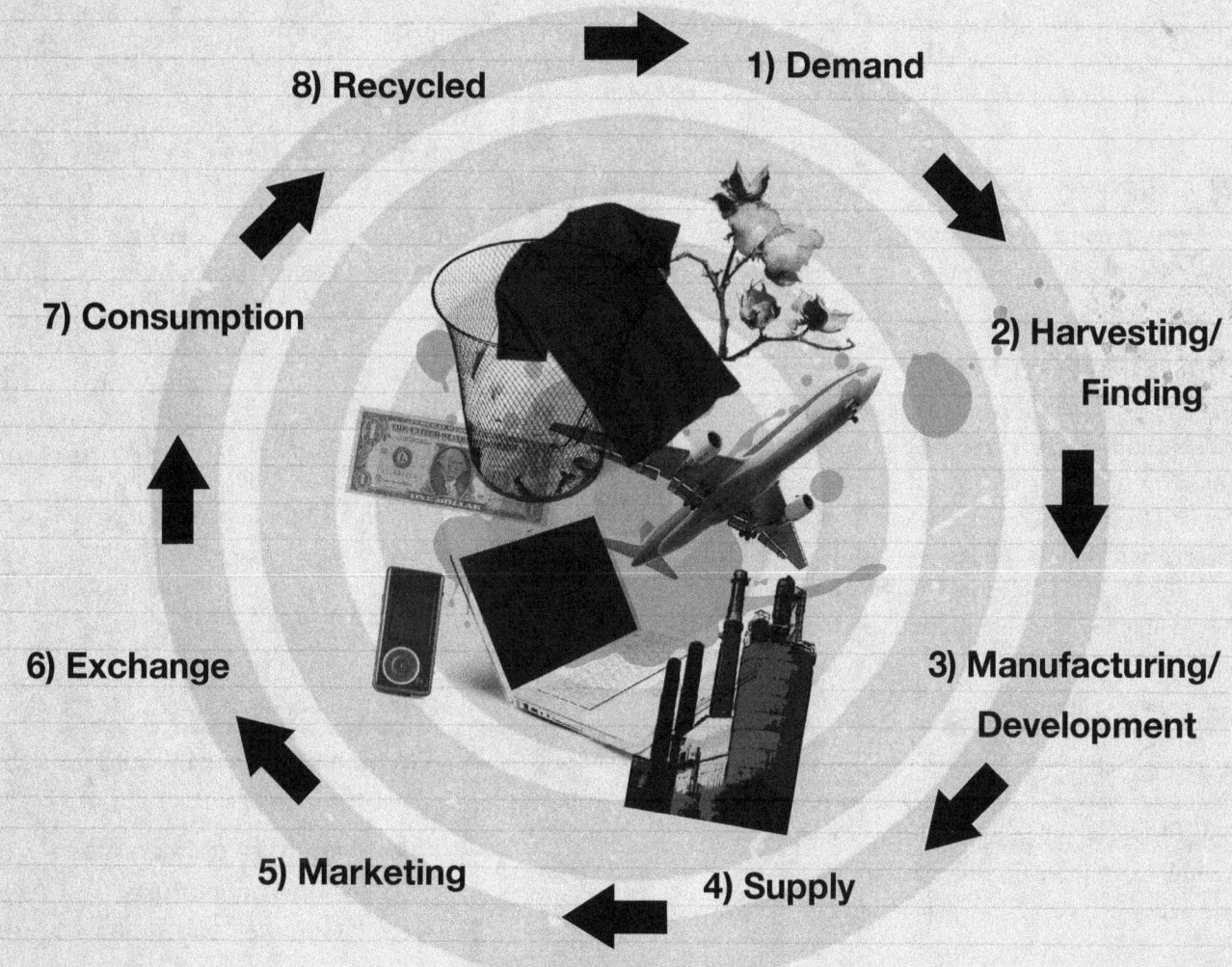

1) Demand
This is the first move in economics. It is where an individual, group, or groups of people have needs and wants, which include the basics of food, water, and shelter. While the *need* for food and water causes stores to stock and supply them for us, there evidently is also a *want* for anything shiny with a small apple logo on it, expensive shoes, fat-burning pills, artificial plants, and other non-priority items, since they are sold all over as well. Demand may also be birthed from human beings' innate creativity, where creative insight into potential innovations develops needs for certain materials and machines to make an idea into a reality.

2) Harvesting/Finding
This is where the demand for any want or need begins to be met. Someone harvests, grows, or finds the raw materials from the earth. For example, crude oil is found deep in the earth, corn is grown on huge lots of land, and gold can be found hidden in rocks, all to satisfy demand.

3) Manufacturing/Development

During manufacturing, raw materials are brought together to make different types of products. Cotton is made into T-shirts, gold into necklaces, corn into corn syrup, steel and plastic becomes a car; the ways raw materials can be used are endless and continue to be expanded upon as innovation progresses.

4) Supply

Once the products and services in demand have been developed, they are supplied to those who demand them. If it's something many people want (like computers or corn), then large quantities are made or grown.

5) Marketing

Though it is not a formal aspect of economic laws, marketing does play a large role between the supply of goods and the people who need them. It is where the suppliers let the public know they have specific goods for sale. Commercials, billboards, advertisements, and mass e-mails are used for this reason. Sadly, much of the advertisements you see everywhere do not simply inform you about products. Often, they are also attempting to persuade you into thinking you need (or demand) their product, where in reality you don't, or at least initially you didn't; this is called manufactured demand. What is worse is when flat out false advertising is used. The best marketing is thoughtful and addresses **consumers** as rational people who can make their own choices.

6) Exchange

Exchange is when the product in demand gets into the hands of the consumer who demands it. The exchange of goods most always involves an exchange of things of equal value. So let us count the cost of what we want by asking the question, "Is this product's cost worth to me what I get out of it?" Is it a fair exchange, or were people abused in the process?

7) Consumption

Consumption is measured when the product or resource is bought. For example, filling the gas tank or buying a new MP3 player is an act of consumption. In economic terms it is why we are, "Consumers," which is a reasonable term except we cannot lose sight of the fact we are human pesons first.

8) Recycled

Truthfully, most of what is bought as a *need* ends up getting thrown away, revealing it to have been a *want* instead. Material possessions do not have the ability to provide lasting happiness as many people seem to think. After the item is purchased, it can become easy for a person to give it, or throw it, away and move on to the next thing, only to become disappointed again; this can lead to a consumerist cycle. But there is a silver lining: because so much good stuff gets dropped off at thrift shops, they are great places to find good deals and may be a good way to slow down the demand for slave labor as well.

Question #2
Which statement would you say is most true?

A) My culture defines me
B) I define my culture
C) I influence my culture and it influences me
D) I have no culture

Question #3
What would be the hardest thing for you to live without?

A) Your favorite clothes
B) Your car
C) Meaning
D) Your reputation
E) Education
F) Friends
G) Family

Zoom in on Supply

The supplying of goods is a wonderful thing. It is one way one person's talents are used to serve others. So first of all, remember to be thankful to those who work so hard to supply things we all need. If people didn't develop and offer their talents, we would not have paved roads, skyscrapers, houses, popcorn, computers, heaters, toilets, or space shuttles.

Regarding slavery, let's connect the dots: Supply is provided because there is demand. This demand, where moral law is ignored, leads to the finding of the world's most vulnerable people and enslaving their mind, body, and soul, in order to satisfy demand. All over the world, humans are taken captive and forced into labor, prostitution, war, and even to give up body organs to satisfy a demand. Getting things that are demanded takes mass unearthing, growing, harvesting, and building, which is also what slaves commonly get forced to do. Few people want to do this kind of hard work; so, many times they force "disposable people" to do it instead.

To be clear, there are a couple of things you should know: not all companies—not even most companies—are bad and guilty of slavery; also, keep in mind that the supply and demand of goods at a fair price is not wrong. Rather, only some demands are gross and morally evil; the trick is for you to learn how to point out such things, and consider distancing yourself from them. The hardest part is to figure out if a product has used human exploitation on its manufacture; ideally, cheap goods would never come at the cost of humans being enslaved or exploited in any form. Try not to merely consider the end result (products and price), but also the means to the end (who, what, when, and where the product was made and how was the environment treated in the process). This establishes the thoughtful consumer, and if all consumers demanded goods produced in ethical ways, that would determine a change in the way products are supplied, and thus abolish the demand for slave labor.

Question #4
Name three pop-cultural norms or values that help promote and feed the demand for sex-focused business.

Zoom in on Demand

In view of human trafficking, what causes the demand for slaves? For some companies, governments, and even unions this is caused by the selfish desire to make more money than they would normally achieve through legal and moral means; but how does that explain sexual slavery? Who are the people behind it, and who are their customers? How does one come to crave non-consensual sex, particularly (and in so many cases) involving children? One way these deformed desires get started is through depraved pornography, which often fuels sexual appetites into huge addictions. This is one way people get into a state of mind that allows for a natural evolution into wishing to own or use a sexual slave. On a deeper level, these activities are mostly fueled by boredom. Without meaning, people begin to look for ways to be fulfilled; depraved sexual fantasies can be one of the choices.

This brings us to sex and the objectification of human beings. Today, sexiness influences a huge portion of the media, be it fashion, music, movies, or even commercials. If we watch some of the current popular music channels for five minutes, for instance, we are likely to see half-naked women with some weird dudes singing about sex and objectifying women. This is not constructive or creative; it aims to get you to want what they've got by preying on your emotions, just like a TV infomercial where the less you think, the easier you can be deceived. We seem to be on a downward trend of objectifying people, which is, in fact, the very stuff that fuels the demand for sexual slavery.

At the end of the day, economic demand is nothing more than a **manifestation** of accumulated desires. These can be desires for things that are good, or for things that are foul. Like it or not, the fact is, people can contribute to the demands for slavery unknowingly. Again, what do you desire? Why? Is that what you should desire?

Let your demand be creative and good.

Question #5
Does it bother you to know slaves, at least partially, make most of what you consume? Circle one

Yes   No   Kind of

If you said yes, what are you willing to do about it?

THINK TANK

Freedom

The fact that all people make choices assumes that all have the **free will** to choose. Freedom is seen as a natural human right all people should have to act, to speak, to feel, or to think as they want, without hindrance or restraint. There are different levels of freedom, with the most basic and deepest one being the inherent personal freedom to think and use reason, which is a freedom no one can take away from us. Political freedom, on the other hand, would be another level of freedom that not every person has.

In human trafficking and slavery, slave owners and traffickers try hard to steal all freedom from people through abuse, drugs, rape, and other forms of violence. They try to eliminate the freedom to use reason from their victims through coercion, trickery and manipulation. The goal is to enslave people not only physically, but mentally. Here, traffickers and slave owners pervert and misuse their freedom by robbing others of their freedoms.

Traffickers forget human freedom does not mean we are free to do whatever we want. People are free to do whatever they want which is morally lawful. For example, we are said to be free, but we are never free to murder; when someone does commit murder, then they have forfeited their right to freedom and it ought to be taken away. This sort of cause and consequence causes most people to try and abide by the law.

The law is not always right, however; in some countries, denying people their right to be free is normal and lawful. It can happen by denying education, maintaining poverty, and permitting the slave trade, among other things. Similarly, in some places it is legal to beat or rape women and children, but this does not make it acceptable. Being able to know what is true and fair, regardless of its lawfulness in a particular country, is the only thing that ensures optimal freedom—which is something that is good for all people and therefore, worth fighting for. The questions for those of us who live in developed countries and have high levels of political freedom are: Are we good stewards of it? Do we take it for granted? Do we only look out for ourselves, or others as well? Are we concerned for our rights only, or also our responsibilities? And finally, do we use our freedom to do good or evil?

Remember that there is no neutral position when choosing between good and evil. Staying neutral is to be neglectful, which is an evil.

Now, let's put on our thinking caps! Locate at least one new resource that discusses freedom. It can be a book, something from the Internet, or a person you talk to, but you should write down what it is and where you found it. Reflecting on the topic, finish by writing a paragraph on the resource you found.

 Creation Tank

A Case Study on Consumerism

Do a video search on the word "consumerism" or "anti-consumerism." Locate a documentary video on this topic and watch it. Then, do an online search on the words metaphysical naturalism, materialism, and narcissism. Define their meanings below and then draw some connections from these philosophical positions to things you learn from the video. As always, do not be spoon-fed rhetoric or propaganda. Instead, be thoughtful about what you hear and read, challenge your personal ideas, and discern the truth from the rubbish where necessary. If you want to go further, consider spending some time thinking about this in light of your culture, personal worldview, and behavior. There is no better time than the present to do some critical thinking and self-examination.

BONUS TASK

For an example of how demands of free people in a free society can bring about exceptional results, go online and find the Ted Talks video, "Anthony Atala: Printing a Human Kidney."

Memoirs of a Young Hero

Be true to yourself, be honest, and write out a few paragraphs. By the end of this book these chapter sections will become the personal and unique story of your journey this far.

Having read through this chapter take some time to write down how what you learned makes you feel and the most important thing you will take with you. Then circle on a scale of 1 to 10 the number that best describes how good of a steward you are with the freedom you have as described in this chapter's Think Tank.

1   2   3   4   5   6   7   8   9   10

Why is this your answer and how do you feel about it? What are some things you can do to move up a few spots? Also, make note of any important "aha" moments you had while going through this chapter.

Journal Lines

Answers: 1) Personal 2) C 3) Personal, but C is the best 4) Personal 5) Personal

CHAPTER 8
MORE MOVES THAN A B-BOY
(THE BIRTHING OF A GLOBAL ABOLITIONIST MOVEMENT)

"Everyone thinks of changing the world, but no one thinks of changing himself."
— Leo Tolstoy

Harriet Tubman

A social movement is a way to describe groups of people who band together to change society in some way. Movements can be bad or good, depending on the direction they take. The Nazi movement was bad and unjust; a movement to abolish slavery would be good and just. Because of its good and just intentions, it can be called a "social justice movement."

Consider something political author Alan Bloom points out in his book, *The Closing of the American Mind*, when talking about social movements of his day: "Commitment, not truth, is believed to be what counts." This is not ideal, yet it is sadly true for a lot of movements, including many today. He goes on, "The radical students of the sixties called themselves 'the movement,' unaware that this was also the language used by young Nazis in the thirties and was the name of a Nazi journal, Die Bewegung. Movement takes the place of progress, which was definite direction, a good direction, and is a force that controls men. Progress was what the old revolutions were evidence of."

Whether we call it progress or a social justice movement based on truth could be a mere matter of semantics. Nevertheless, the point is this: Social justice movements have some common themes. These social themes are listed in the following pages and greatly expanded on in the full-length version of this book if you happen to get a copy. Once we know what needs to be done about human trafficking, we might be able to make a real difference in the world, as long as truth is paramount above all else.

Question #1

Thus far what are the top three most valuable things you've learned from this book?

1)

2)

3)

Why?

This final chapter is where everything learned so far gets tied to action. Most social justice movements have happened within the boundaries of a single country or merely a few countries. Now, however, consider what a worldwide movement might look like. Even better: Another Age of Enlightenment or **Reformation**! We have the education, technology, and talents, so let's start by considering some of the common themes of movements that may apply to our cause:

1. Raising Awareness:

This includes being taught and then teaching others. It also includes advocacy and finding unique ways to inform others. It is one thing to be aware of something, and yet another to actually have understanding of it; therefore, when raising awareness, the largest goal is to offer understanding to those who you talk to. To do this, it is assumed you are prepared to answer questions and offer sound arguments as to why you believe what you do. Further, the success of a social justice movement depends on how consistent it is with human nature, how it advances both rights and responsibilities, and how needed it is.

2. Networking:

Where diverse people with diverse talents join together to promote a shared goal. The hardest part about any social movement can be getting people together, especially if the issue is something widespread, since those who are interested may live far away from each other. The new methods of communication can be very useful when networking.

3. Unifying:

Unifying and organizing people is the next step, once the issue is made public and people are networked. Using the power of words in speeches, sermons, books, and the like can often accomplish this task. To properly unify people, two things are worthy of consideration: First, we must be unified on the truth of the matter and not on the emotions. Emotions change; truth does not. The truth that all people are human beings and deserve to be treated with the same dignity and respect is one of the truths you should stand on. If a movement does not stand on truth, then there is no way to ensure mistakes will not be made, such as with the Nazi movement you read about earlier. Nazis emotionally felt their cause to be just, but in reality were head deep in falsehoods. Second, unity must be organic. There is no sense beating people up with words, appealing to them with pity, or coercing them with "gentle" force to get them involved. Movements are only as strong as their members, and members are only as strong as their commitment; movements that rely on *ad populum* lack integrity and rarely continue standing in the face of intellectual challenges. Our goal is not reached in quantity of members, but in quality of their like-mindedness, grounded in understanding truth. We must not merely go with the flow together, but holistically and intelligently journey the same road.

4. Action:

This is where things can get tricky. Often because social movements serve to disrupt norms, some people don't like them—especially those who support the injustice. Wisdom, courage, and love for mankind, together, can make for a movement that will leave its mark. Building on point three, if our minds are unified, then our actions will also be unified. Appropriate actions ought to be motions to expose and uphold the truth, progressing humankind into greater unity, justice, and peace for a glory that is not their own. If you have ever wanted to get involved in something bigger than yourself, here is your chance!

Question #2
Changing the world for the better is easy.

True   False

Explain your answer.

Question #3
Look up one of these figures that you have never heard of and tell us how they contributed to their respective movements.

A) Dr. Martin Luther King, Jr.

B) William Wilberforce

C) Mahatma Gandhi

D) Desmond Tutu

E) Pick another of your choosing:

Question #4
Which of these do you think you are most suited for?

A) Raising awareness

B) Networking

C) Unifying

D) Action

Question #5
Which step would you say is the most important to have a successful movement?

A) Raising awareness

B) Networking

C) Unifying

D) Action

E) They are all equally important

What would a modern-day, international "abolish slavery and end human trafficking" movement look like? And how would the people involved prove their cause to be right? Could they offer reasonable proof to show why and how slavery and human trafficking are irrational and immoral? While remembering that this is an organic process, and that each of us has a part to play regarding what direction this takes in the future, let us apply the four aspects or attributes of a movement to our cause, and brainstorm a bit:

1. Raising Awareness:

The primary purpose of this book is to raise awareness. By educating you and raising your awareness as its reader, this book serves as a stone thrown in the river; it is now your job to continue raising awareness on other people, and increase the number of ripples in the water.

What you have read so far is not propaganda; rather, it is material seeking to affirm human dignity, yours as well as everyone else's. A global abolitionist's movement has to educate people on the truth of human equality, the wrongness of slavery and human trafficking, and most importantly, its existence in the world. We must draw together philosophy with sociology, and psychology with history, to intelligently communicate to people how slavery is indeed a current worldwide problem, and how we can abolish slavery once and for all.

This also requires us to have an abundance of resources to share. Our movement should include online resources as well as paper resources in every spoken language. In all, each of us has to be prepared before we could ever prepare others; you must know the truth before you can help others see it.

2. Networking:

There are many organizations working right now to abolish human trafficking. This book is presently one very small part. All of these groups might work best if they joined together; there is much work to be done, and things get accomplished quicker if we can share resources. One good idea is to network with groups that possess cultural and national differences from you. When networking, it is important to step outside of your comfort zone whenever possible. By doing this, the message spreads to more places and you can bring new levels of unity to our cause. It also serves to deepen your understanding of human diversity and the beauty therein. In the chapters ahead, you will read about some practical places to start networking, beginning right in your own community. Consider as well all of the ways you can network in an entirely fresh way, through social networking on the Internet and other similar advances.

3 Unifying:

Along with networking, the goal has to be to unify as well. Most importantly, this means to be unified in our reasons for why human trafficking and slavery are wrong. This is where all the talking about human nature, human dignity, social justice, and integrity comes in; if we can all at least agree on these issues, we will be able to change the world for good in a profound way. However, if we disagree on these basic issues, then quite naturally we will also disagree on more complex issues. For example, during the African-American Civil Rights Movement, both Dr. Martin Luther King, Jr. and Malcolm X fought against racism and segregation. However, they did not agree on some of the more basic issues or on what approach to take, so they never worked very closely together. Though the progress they made was legendary, if they had been more like-minded perhaps they could have made even greater progress.

Pay strict attention to how you understand all the facts. Read related books, discuss with each other, and connect up with people close to you who can make the movement better. There is strength in numbers, but numbers are not everything. The more unified we are—first unified within our own individual principals and values, and from this basis, unified as a group—the greater chance we will have to bring down this huge system of oppression.

4 Action:

This could take several different forms: Sophisticated or **grassroots**, political or pop. Through education, networking, and unity, the social justice movement could be global.

Before we apply action to our movement, we must understand we ourselves are the change, which begins with self-examining our beliefs, values, and lifestyles. Only then can we fight for freedom and empower others to reach their potential.

Since action flows naturally from our emotions and thoughts, let us put it all together: If our beliefs about people are true and consistent, then we will have unity; if millions of us are unified in our beliefs, then together our actions will be unified as well, and therefore they will be enormously powerful.

Once the movement gets momentum, many changes will need to happen down the road. To replace slave labor, we may require new inventions and new technology; we will certainly require political changes and policies at every level in every country. We will also require some enlightenment about pornography and the overly sexual pop-culture that helps fuel the fire of the sex slave industry. There are many actions to be taken, but every single one of them starts by taking one small step.

As a word of encouragement and caution, consider the following: Action (or resistance) does not have to be violent! Dr. Martin Luther King, Jr. addressed this many times as an advocate of nonviolent resistance. He said, "The nonviolent resister is just as opposed to the evil act that he is standing against as the violent resister but he resists without violence. This method is nonaggressive physically but strongly aggressive spiritually." He went on to say, "A boycott is never an end within itself. It is merely a means to awaken a sense of shame within the oppressor but the end is reconciliation, the end is redemption." King has numerous pieces of advice which would be beneficial for you to research; if you choose, look up his speeches—The Power of Nonviolence, Pilgrimage to Nonviolence, and many others. Also, see what Gandhi had to say about nonviolence, as he too was an advocate of this tactic and was in fact a big influence on Dr. Martin Luther King, Jr. Information and videos on both of them are readily available online.

THINK TANK

Social Justice

Social justice is not an idea limited to any particular country. It is something found in human nature; because we are equal, we all should be treated as such. Surrendra Gangadean, in his book *Philosophical Foundation* says, "Justice is an ineradicable notion in all human beings requiring equal treatment of equals." Again, if humans were not really equal, then social justice would be an unattainable myth. Because all humans are equal in humanity, we all ought to be treated fairly in justice. However, many people and countries pervert justice to mean something else. To some, justice is by the law of "survival of the fittest," meaning those in power have the right to apply justice as they choose because they are the most fit. And how do you know they are most fit? Well, because they are in power, obviously! We ought not to fall for such blatant trickery. Luckily, many countries have penned the idea that all men are equally under a common law, as they should be.

Justice is no frivolous thing; so that you don't lose its meaning with empty rhetoric, here are three primary things you need to know as you begin to understand the eternal nature of justice:

1) Justice prevents:

Often in the form of laws and rules, justice being served ensures all people are treated fairly and equally. In this case, social justice becomes visible when forms of oppression and exploitation are prevented. The abolition of slavery in the United States is an example of preventative justice: The law is first made to set the standard for justice, and then it gets applied. The best way for justice to be applied is when most (or all) people enforce it; but if people enforce justice on others, they must be sure they themselves are as close as possible to being free of injustice. Since the preventative measures to stop some crimes (such as slavery and human trafficking) have not worked out completely, it is common for some people to take on a defeatist attitude and conclude there is no justice in the world. However, justice exists by the simple fact we all aim to achieve it; it has just not been fully implemented everywhere.

2) Justice corrects:

Corrective justice is seen, for example, in political law systems where breaking laws can lead to being arrested and sent to prison or through other forms of punishment. Basically, if someone acts unjustly, then they are subject to justice being served as a way to correct their actions. In the case of human traffickers, they are breaking all sorts of laws, both legal and moral, against their fellow humans, so justice needs to be served. One important thing to also remember when talking about justice is this: Justice for all includes you and I. Meaning, if we want justice to correct those in error, we must be consistent and accept if it corrects us as well.

3) Justice requires the truth:

Most court systems are established to ensure justice reigns over and against popular belief, power, money, or celebrity status. If laws are not concrete and established any person could change them on a whim, which is not equality, and thus is not just. This might lead to uprising, where people make demands for true justice. Research online the Reformation of the mid 1500's or Gandhi's Salt March in 1929 as examples of people's uprising.

Justice can only rule as far as the truth rules; this is why Americans and many other nationalities must swear "to tell the truth, the whole truth, and nothing but the truth," when giving testimony or taking public office. The very second dishonesty is allowed to exist, justice begins to be corrupted, and that culture could be on its way to being divided and conquered. Ask yourself, "What does 'the truth, the whole truth and nothing but the truth' mean?" Is there a difference between the three terms? Do you actually think there is an absolute truth to be sought or shared? Discuss this with a friend! To help you start, consider this: Is it possible to claim there are no absolute truths without making an absolute statement?

Now, let's put on our thinking caps! Locate at least one new resource that discusses justice. It can be a book, something from the Internet, or a person you talk to, but you should write down what it is and where you found it. Reflecting on the topic, finish by writing a paragraph on the resource you found.

Creation Tank

Born into Brothels

This documentary deals with some troubling stuff, including sex slavery and prostitution, so please get your parents or guardians permission, then go online and track down the documentary *Born into Brothels*. You should be able to find a free version of it. Alternatively, you can go to Shared Hope International and watch their movie called *Demand*. You can find it at: http://www.sharedhope.org. Watch it and then write down your thoughts and feelings about it below, or on the following journal pages.

Memoirs of a Young Hero:

Be true to yourself, be honest, and write out a few paragraphs. By the end of this book these chapter sections will become the personal and unique story of your journey this far.

Having read through this chapter take some time to write down how what you learned makes you feel and the most important thing you will take with you. Then circle on a scale of 1 to 10 the number that best describes how concerned you have been with justice being served equally, as described in this chapter's Think Tank.

1   2   3   4   5   6   7   8   9   10

Why is this your answer and how do you feel about it? What are some things you can do to move up a few spots? Also, make note of any important "aha" moments you had while going through this chapter.

Journal Lines

Answers: 1) Personal 2) False 3) Personal 4) Personal 5) E

20 Forms of Action

1. Buy the book: This is the "Reader" verion of a much bigger book. That one 16 chapters and almost three times as many pages, full of countless ways to reach your highest potential while abolishing modern-day slavery. It even includes an entire section, Action Tanks, designed to help you develop your own forms of action in your community! Buy it and find lots more resources on theworkofkurthoffman.com. Then, start a Young Heroes Club!

2. Begin paying more attention to the places you visit. Is it possible any of the people you encounter could be trafficking victims? Are there any places you might suspect a trafficking victim could be? The United States is home to over 200,000 trafficking victims, around 270,000 in the European Union, and the world at large has at least 27 million, so it is quite possible some victims live near you! If by chance you do discover victims in the United States, please call the national trafficking hotline at 1-888-3737-888, or 911 in an emergency.

Here are some things to look for:

- **Signs of violence or abuse, such as bruises or abnormal fear.**
- **Signs the person is trapped or living where they work**
- **Very young and working long hours**
- **Seem confused and unhappy in their work**
- **Disorientated about where they are, don't speak the local language, and perhaps seem a bit lost**
- **They are working off large amounts of debt to their employer**
- **You can read more at: www.ach.hhs.gov/trafficking**

3. Tell others: Expose the truth about modern-day slavery - in person and through social media. Spread the word about this book on-line and get it into your classroom or after-school program.

4. Invest in change: Support those on the frontlines and enable them to make a difference through fund raising or volunteering.

5. Consume wisely: Hold businesses accountable and ask corporations to join the fight. At www.chainstorereaction.com, e-mail companies to ensure that their products are slave-free. Download Not For Sale's Free2Work Application onto your phone. Check out the SlaveFREE brand. Buying products made by survivors helps ensure their **self-sufficiency** so, shop at the Emancipation Network's www.madebysurvivors.com. Also, consider shopping at Thrift stores, buying other used products at yard sales, used bookstores, and recycling products that are still usable is a great way to help the whole world! If you live in the United States or Canada, go to www.eatwellguide.org to find places in your community where you can get locally grown foods as well.

6. Write: Submit an op-ed. Encourage newspapers, magazines and television stations to publish or to write stories about modern-day slavery, and how to stop it.

7. Map it: Document slavery in your area with the website www.slaverymap.org; pressure law enforcement agencies to make investigations.

8. Make help available: In public places hand out posters, brochures, and other materials about trafficking that can be downloaded from the U.S. Department of Health and Human Services, Polaris Project, and many others.

9. Organize your community to address the issue in your area: For tips on how, visit the following link: www.stopmodernslavery.org/docs/toolkit.pdf

10. Advocate for change: Call or write your elected officials. Tell them that you care about the issue of human trafficking and want stronger laws to protect victims. Keep telling them. Get advice from www.polarisproject.org/take-action on how to engage in political action and advocacy.

11. Be a Good Neighbor: Ask the hard questions in life. Seek truth. Love yourself. Love others. Seriously. It all serves to create a culture where things like slavery cannot coexist.

12. Fight sex tourism: Ask travel agencies, hotels, and tour operators to sign the Code of Conduct for the Protection of Children in Travel and Tourism, found at www.thecode.org. To learn more about sex tourism go to www.justice.gov/criminal/ceos/sextour.html.

13. Prepare caretakers: Encourage healthcare providers and law enforcement officials to be aware of the signs of human trafficking. Download a variety of resource guides from the human trafficking website found in the resource page in the back of the book.

14. Rescue victims: Pressure lawmakers and representatives for raids of forced labor and slavery situations. Lawyers can also make a big difference in advocating for legal investigation and prosecuting perpetrators. Have them join the team at www.ijm.org.

15. Go: Volunteer with organizations caring for survivors. Help build shelters. Teach the local language. Provide skills training. Ask the organization how you can help. Look in the back of the book under the Resources section for a list of many anti-human trafficking organizations currently active in the world today.

16. Slave-Free campuses: Start a group at your high school, college, or university, and make sure your campus is free of products made with slave labor. Start your very own Young Heroes Club!

17. Motivate others: Post links to information on human trafficking, such as the Call + Response movie trailer on your social networking web pages. Encourage your school, church, or organization to use this curriculum, play the Call + Response CD and DVD, or any other materials offered by the various human trafficking organizations. Join the causes of an organization and encourage your friends to do the same.

18. Remember the facts: Memorize the statistics about child and sexual slavery. Tell people.

19. Do what you love: Use your talents to fight slavery. Do an art project and display it in a public place. Use a sports event to raise awareness and funds for the issue. Talk about the issue at a concert, or make it a benefit for survivors. Film a movie on the state of modern-day slavery. Write about the issue and post it on blogs. Start a b-boy dance crew that raises awareness of the issue.

20. Action Tanks: The full-length version of this book comes with 16 Action Tanks across 18 pages giving readers all they need to develop their own form of action in their own community! Get your full-version to start building an epic movement today!

Thanks to Call + Response for compiling a good amount of these forms of action

REASON

APPENDIX II

The following page is a college-level handout designed by Surrendra Gangadean from a Philosophy 101 class.

"Reason" being such a critical and commonly used term, it is notable that a comprehensive definition has never been offered by those who use it. Seeing the need, the purpose of this handout is to provide that critical definition.

As you review it, do not be discouraged if you find parts of it difficult. Almost certainly you will come across terms and ideas that are new to you. Like everything else in this book, however, read, study, question, and seek answers. In all, just recognize it is because all humans have reason that we can say all humans are fundamentally equal and slavery is wrong. If we lose this, all is lost.

REASON : A Comprehensive Definition
Humans have been waiting for about six thousand years for this definition, so enjoy!

Reason can be defined in three ways. First, as what it is in itself; second, as what it is in its use; third, as what reason is, and how we understand and experience it within us.

Consider it …

1. Reason in itself

In itself, reason is the laws of thought. These are:

i) The law of identity: a is a
ii) The law of non-contradiction: Not both a and non-a
iii) The law of excluded middle: Either a or non-a

2. Reason in its use

i) Reason is used to form concepts, judgments and arguments, which are the forms of all thoughts.
ii) Reason is used as a test for meaning; meaning is more basic than truth—if a law of reason is violated, there is no meaning, and wherever there is meaning reason is being used.
iii) Reason is used to interpret (give meaning to) one's experience in light of one's basic beliefs.
iv) Reason is used to construct a coherent world and life view.

3. Reason within us

i) Reason is *natural*: It is not cultural or conventional; it is universal, the same in all persons at all times.
ii) Reason is *ontological*: It applies to being as well as to thought—there are no square circles and no uncaused events.
iii) Reason is *transcendental*: It is authoritative and self-attesting; it cannot be questioned because it makes questioning possible.
iv) Reason is *fundamental*: It is basic to other aspects of human personality; its use is the source of man's greatest good and its denial is the source of man's deepest misery.

Used with permission by the author, Surrendra Gangadean.

REFERENCES

All quotes used with permission by legal right holders, or otherwise, used legally under Fair Use laws

1. Augustine, St. (n.d.). Retrieved from: http://en.wikiquote.org/wiki/Augustine_of_Hippo.

2. Amiel, H.F. (1911) Retrieved from Encyclopedia Britannica (11th ed.), Cambridge University Press.

3. Anderson, O. (2008). Reason and worldviews. University Press of America: Lanham, Maryland.

4. Aristotle, (1885). Politics. Benjamin Jowett translation. Oxford University Press (1905 ed.).

5. Bales, K. (1999). Disposable people. University of California Press: Los Angeles, CA.

6. Bales, K. (2007). Ending slavery: How we free today's slaves. University of California Press: Los Angeles, CA.

7. Bales, K. (2009). The slave next door. University of California Press: Los Angeles, CA.

8. Bales, K. (2005). Understanding global slavery. University of California Press: Los Angeles, CA.

9. Batstone, D. (2007). Not for sale. HarperCollins: New York, NY.

10. Bloom, A. (1987). The closing of the American mind. Simon & Schuster Inc: New York, NY.

11. Douglass F. (1845). The narrative of the life of Frederick Douglass, an American slave. The Anti-Slavery Office.

12. Edison, T. (n.d.). BrainyQuote.com. Retrieved January 8, 2011, from BrainyQuote.com Web site: http://www.brainyquote.com/quotes/quotes/t/thomasaed161979.html

13. Einstein, A. (n.d.). BrainyQuote.com. Retrieved January 9, 2011, from BrainyQuote.com Web site: http://www.brainyquote.com/quotes/quotes/a/alberteins143096.html

14. R.W. Emerson, (n.d.). BrainyQuote.com. Retrieved January 10, 2011, from BrainyQuote.com Web site: http://www.brainyquote.com/quotes/quotes/r/ralphwaldo125383.html

15.   Frankl, V. E. (1959). Man's search for meaning. Boston, MA: Beacon Press.

16.   Gandhi, M. (n.d.). Retrieved from: http://www.avani-mehta.com/2008/08/14/breaking-some-ones-sugar-habit-gandhis-story/.

17.   Gangadean, S. (2008). Philosophical Foundation. University Press of America: Lanham, Maryland. **To maintain the integrity of this author's work please recognize the quotations used are a small part of a large whole. In its entirety, Mr. Gangadean offers a philosophically comprehensive discussion providing answers to a person's most basic questions: "Is knowledge possible and how do we know?" (Epistemology), "What is real?" (Metaphysics), and "What ought we do?" (Ethics). Together these questions combine to make up the whole of all three areas of philosophy. In doing so, Mr. Gangadean expresses the clear connection between how one's epistemological position will influence/determine their metaphysical position, and therefore influence/determine their ethical position as well. For example, one's definition of "human" and "human rights" will be seen in context of how they view human origin and human destiny, which is to say, their metaphysical position. For a further explanation of these ideas please study his book listed here and turn to Appendix II to view his college handout, "Reason."

18.   Garnsey, P. (1996). Ideas of slavery from Aristotle to Augustine. New York, NY: Press Syndicate of the University of Cambridge.

19.   Hale, E. E. (n.d.). Statement published in Year of Beautiful Thoughts in 1902 by Jeanie Ashley Bates Grenough, p. 172, third statement for June 11. Retrieved from: http://en.wikiquote.org/wiki/Edward_Everett_Hale.

20.   Harris, A., & Harris, B. (2008). Do hard things. Colorado Springs, CO: Multnomah Books.

21.   Hunter, Z. (2007). Be the Change: Your Guide to Freeing Slaves and Changing the World. Zondervan: Grand Rapids, MI.

22.   Jefferson, T. (n.d.). BrainyQuote.com. Retrieved January 8, 2011, from BrainyQuote.com Web site: http://www.brainyquote.com/quotes/quotes/t/thomasjeff157211.html

23.   Johnson, B., Gifford, W. (1879). The Works of Ben Johnson. D. Appleton and Company: New York, NY.

24.   King Jr., M. L. (1957). The Power of Nonviolence. Found in: A Testament of Hope: The essential Writings and Speeches of Dr. Martin Luther King, Jr. edited by James M. Washington. Published by Harper Collins in San Francisco in 1986.

25.   King Jr., M. L. (1963). Letter From Birmingham Jail. Found in: A Testament of Hope: The essential Writings and Speeches of Dr. Martin Luther King, Jr. edited by James M. Washington. Published by Harper Collins in San Francisco in 1986.

26. King Jr., M. L. "The Strength to Love." Chapter 14, pt. III. Found in: A Testament of Hope: The essential Writings and Speeches of Dr. Martin Luther King, Jr. edited by James M. Washington, p. 514. Published by Harper Collins in San Francisco in 1986.

27. King Jr., M. L. (1959). The measure of a man. Minneapolis, MN: Augsburg Fortress.

28. King Jr., M. L. (1967). Beyond Vietnam – A Time to Break Silence. In a speech delivered April 4th, 1967. Riverside Church, New York, NY.

29. Lewis, C.S. (1970). God in the Dock. Found in The collected works of C.S. Lewis. Inspirational Press: Edison, NJ. Permissions granted by the Trustees of the Estate of C.S. Lewis.

30. Lincoln, A. (1864). A letter to Albert G. Hodges found in The collected work of Abraham Lincoln edited by Roy P. Basler, Volume VII, p. 281.

31. Longfellow, H.W. (1882). From the Folk-song The Sifting of Peter in Ultima Thule. Riverside Press: Cambridge, MA. Retrieved from http://books.google.com.

32. Mann, H. (1838). Journal entry October 29. Retrieved from: http://en.wikiquote.org/wiki/Horace_Mann.

33. Maslow, A. H. (n.d.). Maslow quote found at: BrainyQuote.com. Xplore Inc, 2011. 4 January. 2011. http://www.brainyquote.com/quotes/quotes/a/abrahammas159012.html

34. Maslow, A. H. (1954). Motivation and personality, Harper and Row: New York, NY.

35. Meltzer, M. (1993). Slavery, A World History. Da Capo Press New York, NY.

36. Roosevelt, F.D. (1936). From his acceptance speech for the re-nomination for the Presidency, Philadelphia, Pa. June 27.

37. Rousseau, J.J. (1762). The social contract. Reprinted by Cosmio books: New York, NY. Retrieved from: http://books.google.com/.

38. Santayana, G. (1920). The Life of Reason or the phase of human progress. Charles Scribner's sons: New York, NY.

39. Schaeffer, F. A. (1968). Escape from Reason. Downers, IL: Inter-Varsity Press.

40. Socrates. Apology, 38a. Retrieved from: http://en.wikiquote.org/wiki/Socrates

41. Spencer, H. (1901). From a letter to Sir Robert Giffen. Retrieved on January 7, 2011 from: Those who enslave other peoples enslave themselves.

42.   Strauss, W. & Howe, N. (2003). The Fourth Turning. Broadway Books: New York, NY.

43.   Thurman, H. (n.d). Retrieved from: http://en.wikipedia.org/wiki/Howard_Thurman

44.   Tolstoy, L. (1900). Appears in latter form in Pamphlets. Translated from the Russian (1900) Leo Tolstoy, Free Age Press, Maldon, Essex, p. 29. Retrieved from: ww.wikiquote.org.

45.   Tocqueville, A. (1856). The Old Regime and the French Revolution, 3.3, 1856, tr. Stuart Gilbert, 1955

46.   Twenge, J.M. (2006). Generation Me: Why Today's Young Americans are More Confident, Assertive, Entitled – and More Miserable than Ever Before. Free Press: New York, NY.

47.   United States Declaration of Independence, The. Found at http://www.ushistory.org/declaration/document/.

48.   United States Constitution, The. Found at http://www.usconstitution.net/const.html

49.   Washington, B.T. (1904). Quoted in Charm and Courtesy in Conversation by Frances Bennett Callaway in 1904, p. 153. Retrieved from: www.wikiquote.org.

50.   Washington, B.T. (1909). An address on Abraham Lincoln before the Republican Club of New York City. Retrieved from: http://en.wikiquote.org/wiki/Booker_T._Washington

51.   Wiesel, E., (1958). Night. Hill and Wang: New York, NY.

* Note: This is the entire Reference list from the complete book, *Young Heroes: A Learner's Guide to End Human Trafficking*. Not all names listed here appear in this Reader! version. Just FYI...

SHOUT-OUTS!

Big thank you to my wife who supported me in writing this book. It means everything to me; you are exceptional! And to my mother who managed to keep her sanity while raising such a wild kid! You're always had my back.

Thank you to all those who have helped me develop and/or pilot this resource! Becky Ankeny, Katie and Mark at Arizona League to End Regional Trafficking; the Girl Scout GEMS in Phoenix; Ian and Noel at Neighborhood Ministries; Stephen at the BBC; the girls at Peer Solutions; Nelson S.; Jeff and Lexi at Jonas and Treat Photography, Cora at Cubis Media; and big huge thanks to Becky at Becky Ankeny Design, who sacrificed many days to help design the layout of this book. Also, thanks to editors, Korah, Jason K., Jason M., Teri, Kevin Bales and his son Gabriel, Kelly B, as well as, Angela at my former publishing house who provided the refining fire I needed to become better. And to the original mind-blower.

Lastly, thanks to all of the young heroes who helped me along the way as well! Catalina, Nathan, Robie, Alex, Philip, Russel, Jessica, Jamie, Sergio, Carlos, Shantea, Nidy, Rachel, Alexis, Brandon, and all the rest! I appreciate you all for your selfless acts of kindness and service!

ABOUT THE AUTHOR

At every parent-teacher conference Kurt's Mother heard the exact same thing – he has great potential but no interest in reaching it. Kurt himself will tell you, he absolutely hated school - because he never understood the big "why" questions about life, knowledge, and education. A little late to the party, Kurt nevertheless strived through various struggles to learn the life-giving joy and value of knowledge, going on and graduate with three degrees: an Integrative Studies Bachelor's in Philosophy and Counseling, a Master's in Social Work, and a Master's in Public Administration. Effectively blowing the minds of his former teachers Kurt's story also demonstrates to the world that even struggling, hurt, and misguided youth are brimming with potential - a potential that is cultivated in and through the pursuit of finding answers to life's hardest questions and knowledge of one's inherent human dignity.

Now living in Jackson, Michigan with his beautiful wife and three amazing kids, Kurt is an Assistant Professor of Social Work at Spring Arbor University where he enjoys educating and empowering young and adult learners to change themselves and the world for the good. To learn more please visit drummerboybooksandmedia.com.

We are more than excited to be a part of this amazing book and the several more Young Heroes Books to come.